ABOUT THE AUTHOR

Ron has been a writer, director and producer of over 100 television documentaries and newscasts in New York, Hollywood and London, and has produced critically-acclaimed live performance shows, such as *Meet Thomas Jefferson*. Ron has also served as Adjunct Professor at several universities and technical schools, teaching communications, writing and staging. He is President of the Nonverbal Institute.

Ron got his start in television broadcasting at WJIM TV in Lansing, Michigan as a director, producer and on-camera host of various television shows, including children's shows. He worked for the Jackie Gleason Show in New York and with Allen Ludden in Hollywood on the creative development staff. Ron also provided nonverbal consulting to various movie directors and producers at Pinewood Studios in London.

Ron received his Bachelor's Degree in Television Broadcasting and his Master's Degree in Communication (with the focus on Nonverbal Communication) from Michigan State University, and studied neurolinguistics (the abstract knowledge of language) at Stanford University. Ron also studied pantomime under the French Master, Marcel Marceau, and as a result, became totally immersed in the art and science of body language. He has focused over 30 years in research, training and lecturing on this vital subject, and this book is an accumulation of a lifetime of knowledge teaching nonverbal communication.

Ron's company, the Nonverbal Institute, specializes in the teaching of nonverbal communications and body language. His clients range from corporate executives, sales managers, and human resource managers, to real estate agents, health care workers, and federal government employees. Ron works as a public speaker, private consultant, and advisor. He may be reached at www.nonverbalinstitute.com.

ACKNOWLEDGEMENTS

The author expresses his appreciation to the thousands of people he has quietly studied in various walks of life and to the many people he has coached one-on-one showing them their positive and negative nonverbal signals. Special thanks go to my sons, John and David, who have helped me throughout my career; also, acknowledgement to my other children who have encouraged my love of this fascinating subject. I am very grateful to Anita, my wife and Director of Operations, who handles the details for all of my talks, seminars and coaching.

My earliest inspiration came from Marcel Marceau, the famous French pantomimist who came to this country in the late 50's and sponsored a pantomime contest in New York City. As one of the winners, I was able to study under him for three weeks. This study changed my life. I began to wonder about gestures, facial expressions, movement, eye contact and so much more. Monsieur Marceau and I became friends and we appeared on many local television shows around the country with my poor French helping his poor English. This experience prompted me to pursue a Master's Degree in communication at Michigan State University with a focus on nonverbal communication.

I thank Professor Randall Harrison and of MSU's Communication Department who helped me to see the scope of this subject. Thanks to my research assistant, Suzanne Brown from the Marion County Library. Many thanks to Professor Ray Birdwhistell of the University of Pennsylvania, whose expertise and generosity commanded my attention to make this subject a continual focus in my life. I offer special thanks to the former President of Southern Virginia University, Monte Nyman, who has always been one of my best audiences on this subject. And to my father, Darwin Lewis Grow who had an amazing ability of reading people's nonverbal signals instantly on his first meeting. This author grew up thinking all fathers could take one look at a person and know a great deal about them. This inherited gift has helped my work in this field extremely well. And finally to the Holy Ghost, who prompts me with feelings, insights and understandings about the sweet people I coach.

Communication between two people has become extremely complicated by all the signals we are bombarded by; nevertheless, human communication begins and ends for this writer in nonverbal signals. As Robert Frost said, "a poem can never be translated accurately"; neither can nearly all nonverbal signals.

By increasing the reader's ability to understand nonverbal signals more effectively, this book should increase more effective communicators. I also recognize my editor Dave Clements. What can I say about a man who demanded clarity, proper segues and eliminating redundancies, vagueness and unnecessary pages? His myopic focus added enormously to my difficulties of removing my 'best' unrelated paragraphs. What can I say about this torture and painful experience? Thanks for every minute of it.

Ronald Lewis Grow
Summerfield, FL

CONTENTS

INTRODUCTION

"When you are in the presence of another human being, you cannot __not__ communicate." [1]

An extraordinary statement, but it is absolutely true. People send out nonverbal signals every waking moment, whether they are aware of it or not. When these silent signals are recognized by people who understand their meaning, they communicate messages; some weak, others more prominent.

This book started in the late 1960's when I gave my first talk on nonverbal communication and when I had my first counseling session with eleven Vice Presidents of Oldsmobile, Division of General Motors in Lansing, Michigan. Except for a few sojourns into television, films, pantomime stints and an enjoyable task of interviewing almost ninety Human Relations Directors, I have been almost full time in nonverbal communications, and since 1990, I have been almost exclusively focused on this fascinating subject. It has been a great pleasure. I hope this book reflects the good I have done and the blessings I have been able to give salespeople, management and resource people.

A Princeton Professor and distinguished author once commented that writing a book is like building an ice berg. The book part is only one-seventh (or that part which can be seen and read). Most of the subject for the author's book is unseen—the six-sevenths of the contents which are under the water. One of the biggest problems faced by most authors is what to leave out. This certainly fits this subject, and there was much information that my editor wisely choose to remove.

---

1   Nonverbal Behavior in Interpersonal Relations, Richmond & McCroskey, 75 Arlington Street, Suite 300, Boston, MA 02116, 2004, page 4

This book will explain the major nonverbal signals that most people use, and I will offer anecdotal examples placed throughout the book. Most of these anecdotes will follow detailed explanations of a certain signal. Understanding the potential meanings of how these signals positively and negatively affect interpersonal communications can give the reader an increase in communication power.

I also hope to add to the knowledge about this fascinating subject, although probably one book in ten contains anything new in either knowledge or imagination, and most have been rewriting Julius Fast's book *Body Language*, originally published in 1970.

WHERE THIS BOOK STARTED

MARCEL MARCEAU - HIS MESSAGES WENT ALL OVER THE WORLD BUT HE NEVER SPOKE A WORD

As mentioned in the acknowledgements, my earliest inspiration came from Marcel Marceau, the famous French pantomimist who came to this country in the late 1950's and sponsored a pantomime contest in New York City. As one of the winners, I was able to study under him, and this opportunity changed my life. I began to wonder about gestures, facial expressions, movement, eye contact and so much more. Monsieur Marceau and I became friends and we appeared on many local television shows around the country; my poor French helping his poor English. This experience prompted me to pursue a Master's Degree in communication at Michigan State University.

One afternoon in a dance studio at the University of Michigan, Monsieur Marceau spent most of an afternoon explaining how the movement (and frozen position) of the face, eyebrows, eyes, lips, mouth, and head were the major components enabling the audience to know what someone was feeling—and what message they were conveying. He demonstrated this in a myriad of ways with his pliable face (highlighted by makeup). The genius of this man's talent seemed to focus on the power of his face.[2]

---

2   Marcel Marceau believed the face was the most important part of the body in sending the message of a mime.

Marcel stood behind a screen where only his face was seen. His body was hidden. He froze his face in an expression and we had only a few seconds to write down the message we believed was being communicated. We were to write down two things: the feelings or emotions in one column and the main facial signal or message in the second. An example would be the *feeling of happiness* and the main <u>signal</u> might be *smiling*. It turned out to be an extraordinary exercise.

Marcel presented about fifteen frozen face signals. Approximately thirty students and two professors were in the room and every single one of us wrote down the same words for every facial expression. All of us were surprised by our unity. How did this happen? Why did we all write the exact words down about Marcel's facial expression? The genius of this man's talent seemed to focus on the power of his face.

One professor asked Marcel, "If I did those same expressions, do you believe our class would have all written the same words?" Marcel's answer was if you place your face muscles in the right places, and held them, all citizens of the world would recognize the same messages.

THE COMMUNICATION OF YOUR FACE
COMES FROM YOUR HEART

A student then said, "So it's the muscle in our faces which communicates." Marcel, almost angrily yelled out his answer, "No! No! Vous devez sentir l'expression dans votre Coeur." Translation: "No! No! You must feel the expression in your heart." The translation of his next statement was, "Communication of your face comes from your heart." He added that everyone wrote the same words down on the paper because his message came from his heart and not his face muscles. He added that if he hadn't felt the expression in his heart, then everyone would have written something different.

The next demonstration Marcel did was to reveal only his body. His face was hidden. He held about fifteen body positions (each conveying a signal) for a few seconds and again we wrote down the feeling and then the message or signal for that body position. An example would be a *feeling of boredom* and *slumped or poor posture* for the signal. Of the entire class, only three or four got similar answers. This exercise proved to be useless. Marcel said over and over "Sans le visage, notre message nous sans signification." Translation, "Without the face, our body message is meaningless." For me it meant that without the facial nonverbal signals most body signals were difficult to read.

If the class had ended then and there, it was worth a lifetime moment, but Marcel would add more insight to his mimes and, for me, to the silent messages of interpersonal communication.

In his next demonstration, Marcel revealed only his neck and arms and hands, but no face, head or legs. He froze several positions focusing mainly on his hands and arms each time. He would place his 'arms and hand muscles' (his language) in a locked position and asked again to write down what feeling and what signal we saw. For most of us, the arms and hand signals were the second easiest feelings and signals to read or comprehend. More than half of the class got the feelings, fewer got the signals.

For the last demonstration, Marcel revealed his entire body and repeated many of the previous signals. No one missed any of them. It was an artist and entertainer's approach to his craft showing us the power of the face muscles and the contributions of those messages with the rest of the body.

In the afternoon session he did several of his great pantomimes. This day at the University of Michigan I will never forget as it changed my life forever.

Marcel Marceau and I became part time 'grand partenaire' as he and I would meet at various theater venues in Detroit Universities and both of Michigan's great universities. At the University of Michigan he considered putting his International School of Pantomime, but the French Government said no. Marceau was a demanding perfectionist at each venue where he performed. He said every detail had to be spoken. There was no silent communication in staging his two hour show.

My life in nonverbal communication was impacted again in San Quentin Prison; not as an inmate, but where I began this life-time study in nonverbal communication.

TWO INMATES OF SAN QUENTIN PRISON

While in graduate school at Michigan State University, I was informed that Professor Ray Birdwhistell (one of my favorite scholars on this subject) was going to teach a summer class on nonverbal communications at Stanford University. Two Professors from MSU were also going to attend Birdwhistell's classes. Coincidentally, CBS TV was going to cover the Presidential Nominating Convention at the Cow Palace in 1964. I was asked by Bill Gordon of CBS Affiliates, at CBS in New York, if I would like to be a volunteer runner for CBS at that convention. This meant that I could also take a television course at Stanford. Since I was already out in Northern California for the summer, I jumped at the offer, and enrolled in the television course and was permitted to attend Birdwhistell's seminar.

While in Palo Alto, Michigan State professors Randall Harrison and Professor D. Kagan had arranged to videotape the prison counselor at San Quentin Prison for more studies in nonverbal communication. I was invited to attend this video taping session. The following event changed my life.

Professor Harrison asked the counselor if we could also video tape the inmates. It is important to know that the warden did NOT want this video taping to take place. So he sent us two who probably were the worse inmates in the prison population. It turned out to be the best thing he did for us. One was a 20 year prison inmate who was purposely mute; he rarely said anything to anybody. The other most likely was the main bully and fight instigator in the prison population. He was a large and imposing threat to all of us.

FIRST INMATE: COUNTING HIS BROTHERS

The mute inmate was asked if he had any brothers. He answered "four". Name them was the question. NOW…IT IS NOT WHAT THE INMATE SAID THAT WAS IMPORTANT…BUT WHAT HE DID…HIS NONVERBAL SIGNALS.

The inmate counted his brothers on his left hand fingers, using his right hand's index finger to touch each of his left hand fingers as he said, "There's Tom… Dick… Harry and…

For his last brother the inmate did NOT touch the forth finger, BUT counted his last brother by jabbing his closed right hand with the thumb pointing out (with the same gesture an umpire would call a man out at the plate in baseball). Professor Kagan and I saw this odd hand signal of the right hand. Why didn't the inmate count his last brother on his last finger of his left hand?

Kagan slipped a note to the counselor to ask the same question again. In a few minutes he asked the inmate to name his brothers again. The inmate did the exact same nonverbal signal…throwing his right hand thumb out in the air as he named "Jimmy," his younger brother.

This interesting hand signal could have meant nothing, but Doctor Kagan and I wanted to know why the inmate had singled out his younger brother Jimmy.

Doctor Kagan interrupted the counselor and asked many questions about Jimmy. Remember, this inmate hated to talk.

But for some reason, the inmate started talking non-stop about his younger brother Jimmy. We learned when the inmate did something good as a young boy, Jimmy got credit for it. When the younger brother did something bad, the inmate was blamed. This inmate grew up hating his younger brother.

Hate is the heaviest baggage we will ever carry. The amazed counselor was surprised by the inmate's willingness to talk and continued to get more information about the inmate's obvious problem with his younger brother.

SECOND INMATE: HE MOVED HIS WEDDING RING BACK AND FORTH…WHY?

Then it was the bully's turn at the table. This muscle man bully played to the camera and it was very difficult to get him to settle down and answer the counselor's questions. The bully was totally in charge of the interview, swearing, finding fault with the camera lights in the room and generally very disruptive.

The counselor's questions were never answered. We were getting nowhere and were about to wrap it up when the counselor asked, "Tell me about your wife." The bully became louder and a little scary as he gave a glowing summary of his wife. She was pretty, faithful; everything was fantastic.

However, all the time he was talking about his wife, the bully gave conflicting nonverbal messages, shaking his head back and forth while saying how wonderful she was; throwing his hand out as he mentioned things she did which were "really nice".

It turned out that the most significant signal was moving his wedding ring up and down his finger…in a nervous manner. Kagan, Harrison and I all saw these conflicting signals and wanted to see if the truth was someplace else.

The counselor started to wrap up the session when Dr. Kagan, leaning close to the bully, said directly and very slowly, "Why don't you tell us the truth about your wife?"

That statement stunned the bully. He froze. He seemed to deflate right before our eyes. He became submissive; a little scared and said nothing more.

Dr. Kagan asked again, "Tell us the truth about your wife."

In a softer voice he then told us a horror story about his wife. (NOTE: nearly every inmate blames "his old lady" for being in prison). But the bully seemed totally honest; his verbal now agreed with his nonverbal. He gave us details, which seemed to come out of a broken heart. The bully then paused and the room was very quiet for a long time.

Dr. Kagan was the first one to speak…in a very soft voice, "I believe you."

After a long pause with his eyes tearing up the former bully asked, "What?"

"I believe you…she sounds like a terrible person," said Dr. Kagan. The bully deflated even more and the tears were flowing. The room was silent for a long time. This bully was now a different human being, transformed right before our eyes…all because Dr. Kagan noticed a nonverbal signal which, in this case, meant something.

Soon the inmates were back in their cells and we were saying our goodbyes. Little else was said. We had all experienced a catharsis because of two very interesting nonverbal moments. The counselor left without saying more than "Thanks, it was extraordinary."

The conclusion of this story came from the Warden almost a year later. We heard that the first non-talkative inmate made parole the next time it came up and the bully never caused another fight in the population. Apparently, he even apologized for giving us a hard time that warm, summer day. That was the day I knew that I wanted to learn, counsel, teach, and make a living in the world of nonverbal communication.

Through the use of written words in the previous account of the two inmates, you witnessed how a flagrant gesture and a not-so-subtle gesture triggered the observers to make further inquires of the inmates. You might think of it as *What Are They Really Saying?*

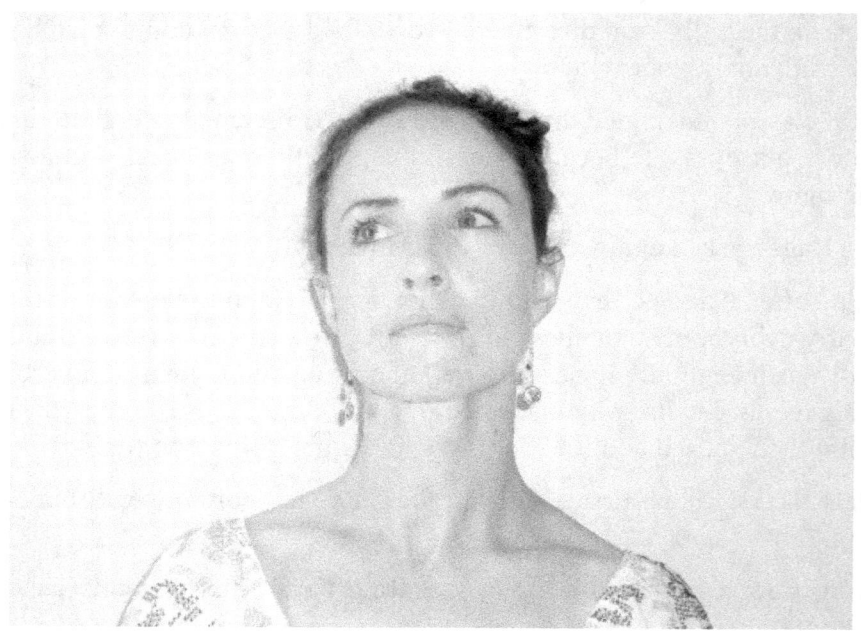

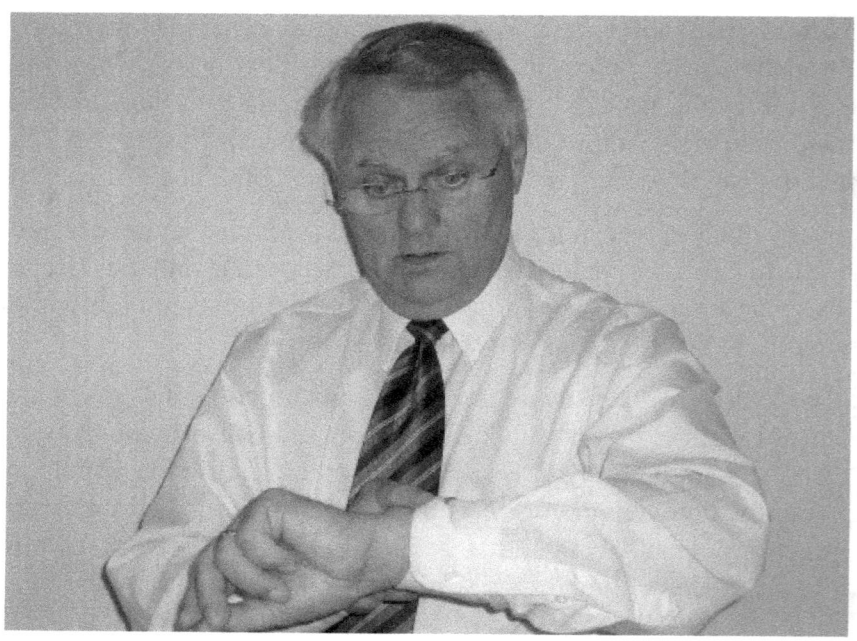

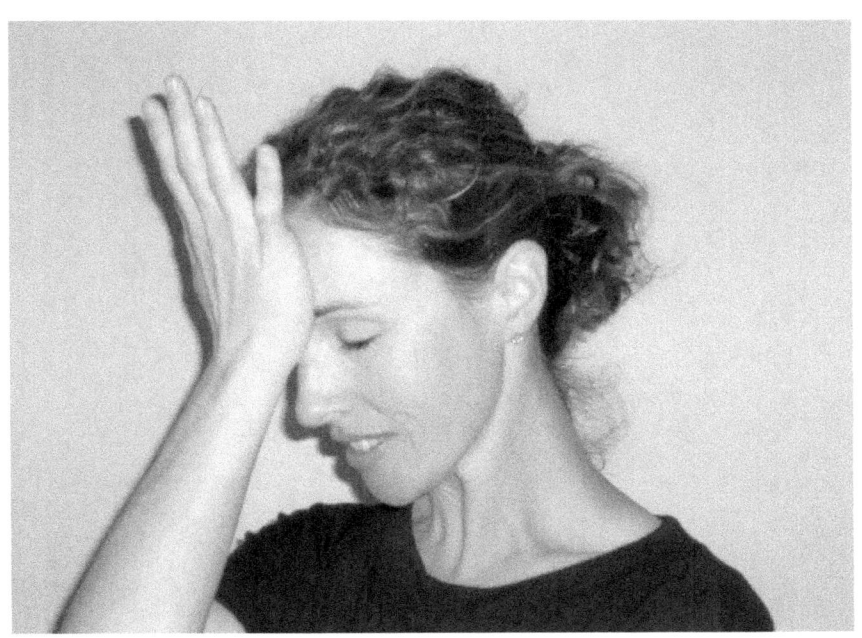

CHAPTER 1

MY NONVERBAL LABORATORY

The location for studying nonverbal signals is not a mouse filled lab nor the book-lined shelves of Stanford. Greek history never mentioned the subject. As far as this writer knows, the first interesting books on this subject began in the mid twentieth century. For me, my laboratory has been in management offices, sales situations, Human Resource offices, in front of parents, married couples and among people of other cultures. Wherever I have traveled, I have found important nonverbal signals being displayed under countless different circumstances.

THE CLASSROOM SPEAKS

A consensus held by many university professors, and as a former adjunct professor I have experienced this many times myself, we usually know after the first class session if we have a good group of students or not. It doesn't take long to have a sense about what kind of class we will have for 14 weeks, and this information comes from the students' nonverbal signals. When a student arranges his or her books neatly on the desk and sits up straight with good eye contact, usually this student will show up on time, participate in class, and do better on tests. If we see students with no books, sitting a little sideways, perhaps aiming their feet at the door, and busy texting on their cell phones or with their heads turned away so there is little eye contact, we pretty well know that this student will only show up occasionally, have average grades and rarely participate in class. There are exceptions, but not many.

INTUITION IS ALSO A CLASSROOM FOR NONVERBAL KNOWLEDGE

Most people have not studied nonverbal communications academically, yet they have an intuitive awareness of its existence by the way people show or "speak" through their body language.

Mothers for example, will question a young child who has just come home from school and notices that her child's facial expression bears nonverbal signals indicating that something is troubling the child.

A perceptive boss may notice that a healthy employee is moving slower and slouching during a meeting in which the employee is usually attentive. In these two situations, the untrained mother and boss are observers of unspoken communication.

The basis of recognizing these obvious nonverbal signals are testimony that we have the fundamental skills necessary to take an even more in-depth study into the dynamics of nonverbal communication.

As you will learn, there are a multitude of nonverbal signals that speak silently about peoples' circumstances. The circumstances and the nonverbal signals that are allied with them are far reaching. I propose to teach you how to recognize, understand, and interpret these nonverbal signals so that you can have an advantage in everyday interpersonal communications. I call this 'a communication advantage'.

I have been teaching communication advantages to salespeople, managers, CEO's, Human Resource Directors, teachers, parents and medical personnel for most of my adult life; people just like you.

CHAPTER 2

GET THE COMMUNICATION ADVANTAGE

THE SIX FOCUSES OF THIS BOOK:
SELLING • INTERVIEWING • HIRING • MANAGEMENT
PARENTING • IMPROVING SELF ESTEEM

More nonverbal signals are missed than read correctly, and most people say more by their nonverbal signals than by all the words that they speak.

The publishing of another book on nonverbal communication or body language is written with the personal view that new information is still available. I am reminded of the great English essayist, De Quincey, who wrote in the 1850's, "…only one book in ten thousand contains anything new in the realm either of knowledge or imagination. All the rest are to be classed as repetitious and commentaries. The genuine creations of the human mind are few."[1]

An English Professor friend of mine mentioned that of all the poems Emerson wrote, only five lines remain after sifting.

This book offers a completely different view of nonverbal signals than the focus of many authors and researchers in this field. It is for people in sales, marketing, human resources professions, and for anyone else for whom better understanding of what people are *really saying* is critical. It can also help management leaders, and help you to be a better parent or spouse. With many years of counseling, I can also say without hesitation, it can improve your self esteem.

---

1   The Masterpieces and the History of Literature, Julian Hawthorn, Vol 1, E.R. DU Mont, 1903, Preface

A SAMPLING OF THE
COMMUNICATIVE ADVANTAGE

Understanding nonverbal signals gives a person a major communicating advantage and even communication power. Being aware of these signals *will* help you and give you an advantage. Missing or misunderstanding these powerful signals will limit your communication success!

Let's examine a common situation in which the sales person (we will call him Joe) is making a sales pitch to a prospect, and Joe thinks he has covered all the possible questions the prospect may have. However, Joe has talked non-stop and never sees one of the most important nonverbal signals from the other person. The prospect has just taken a breath through their mouth. Assuming this person does not have a nasal congestion, this signal of taking a breath through the mouth (almost always) means they want to ask a question or say something. But Joe didn't see that important signal and keeps on talking. The prospect is not granted a moment to speak, becomes frustrated, gives up listening, and Joe – he lost the sale. We can speculate about what the prospect may have wanted, but that signal was missed….and so was the sale.

Human Resource Directors' interviewing and hiring skills for their company positions can be greatly improved if they know what nonverbal signals to look for.

Too many Human Resource Directors hire the wrong people, and all of the evidence not to hire them was available in the first interview; but the interviewer missed these important signals. These mistakes can cost companies a great deal of lost revenue.

In businesses where the 'front-line' person or the first person your potential customer or prospect sees is an extremely important person. Think of hotels, motels, convenient stores and other businesses where the wrong person at the counter inadvertently drove a customer away; never to return again. In today's culture this problem is widespread and the evidence of poor hires is on every block.

How would you like to hire a person who, during the interview process, gave you a facial expression that looks like some of the following pictures?

"What else does this job require?"

"That really sounds interesting."

"Yes, I've done that before."

"Well, I think that's true."

CHAPTER 3

FACTS - FICTION - DISCLAIMER

Since the first book published on nonverbal communication in the early 20th century, there has been a plethora of misinformation printed about nonverbal messages. These books frequently are summaries of someone else's research. Too many were written for other scholars.

The subject matter has fluctuated from Body Language to Nonverbal Communications to Neurolinguistics and back again to Body language.

Too many authors of this subject have expanded the subject to register precise meanings to certain nonverbal signals thereby creating black and white interpretations of them. This approach has polluted the field of study with falsehoods, exaggerations and nonsense.

For instance, when you see someone rubbing his or her nose, it *could* mean they are feeling and thinking 'no' or they're lying (see chapter 25). It could also mean their nose itches. Lying causes the chemical catecholamine to be released which causes tissue inside the nose to swell and nerve endings to itch. So liars will usually rub their noses or face.[1]

If these misleading authors had modified or footnoted their claims with the words 'possibly…maybe…on some occasions…might mean', then their books would have more value. So be advised.

---

1   *The Definitive Book of Body Language*, Allan Pease, Bantam Dell, Div. of Random House, Inc.

CHAPTER 4

WHAT IS
NONVERBAL COMMUNICATION ?

Can one gesture mean a thousand words?

One of the oldest of all ancient temple documents, the Shabako Stone says, "...the way one becomes a member of the universe is through one's sensory perceptions. Whatever gets us from out there must come through 'the seven gateways', the eyes, ears, nose, taste buds, touch, speech *and* the mouth."[1] Every book on this subject attempts to define the subject of nonverbal communication; they all make similar definitions.

The definition of nonverbal communication or body language will differ from anthropologists, sociologists and ethnologists. But most communication professors and public speaker consultants pretty much agree. Anything on this earth which communicates a message or feeling without words is nonverbal communication. It includes everything from: *facial expressions to a tooth ache, the message of a massage to the playful pinch, dance to drama, mime to a painting, fashion to fad, the smell of roses to the taste of a steak, the world trade disaster to the stubbing of the toe, a sun setting to a sun burn.*

Our brain works both nonverbally and verbally and can convert messages seen, felt, heard and tasted into verbal messages extremely fast. Many, including this consultant, but not all are nonverbal thinkers or visualizes. There will be many readers of this book who are verbal thinkers or verbalizers. I know a few people who are both verbalizers and visualizers. It is reasonable to assume that both the nonverbal and

---

1   The Book of Formation, Sefer Yetzirah) Knut Stenring, tr., London: Rider and Son, 1923, p 27-28 Shabako Stone, line 56

verbal component of communication are often necessary for a receiver to get the entire message and understand the meaning behind it.[2]

However, if the exchange of information through nonlinguistic signs, feelings and signals are to have any value, someone must see them. As we shall see, nonverbal signs can be seen by humans, animals and it seems, even insects.[3]

There is an enormous amount of nonverbal communication going on around us. It is MORE than the written and spoken words combined. Most of the time, these nonverbal signals are seldom or never seen by many people.

The internet has become a major communication of words, pictures, feelings and information. Someone somewhere is probably writing a book how nonverbal signals are a major part of these messages and how they are connected to this Twenty First Century. For sure, nonverbal signals will always be a major and significant part of interpersonal communication.

Understanding nonverbal signals should help us to be more efficient and more effective in our face-to-face communication. We should communicate with less effort, in less time and with fewer misunderstandings. Learning about these signals is a continuous and growing opportunity.

The modern era of empirical nonverbal research probably began in the 1970's. And it was in 1971 that one of the best books on this subject was written by Randall Harrison.[4] Nearly everyone has some idea what nonverbal signals are. Most will say nonverbal communication or body language equals expressions and leave it there. Others will include eye contact, and maybe hands (which are gestures). Few will mention posture, body movement or the clothes they are wearing. Nonverbal communication is the component form of human commu-

---

2   Nonverbal Behavior in Interpersonal Relations, Richmond & McCroskey, Pearson Education, Inc. 75 Arlington St., Suite 300, Boston, MA 02116, p. 5. Nonverbal behavior should not be confused with nonverbal communication. One is a signal emitting information and the other is a certain behavior perhaps initiated by this signal.
3   Nonverbal Communications, Randall P. Harrison, Michigan State University Press, 1974 P 11 Flora Davis writes, "A child will recognize NVS better as a child than as an adult."
4   Ibid, p.11

nication in which speaking is manifested through various body, face, and gesture signals.[5]

It is amazing that from the first book published in 1959 through 1980, bibliography devoted to nonverbal research had more than 4,000 references. By 1970 nonverbal research expanded at an exponential rate. For this author too much of it was about sexual relations, dating signals and improving ones sensuality. Today we have many monthly and quarterly publications on the subject.[6] I do not hesitate to add one more publication knowing it will be read by more than read Isaac Newton's Principia Mathematica. Most believe less than ten people on earth (at that time) could read that book.[7]

Nonverbal signals might be thought of as the background music in a movie drama. The background music suggests to the observer that a feeling is attached to the scenario, in this case, the dialogue. Also, the background music can be thought of as the underlying elements of the movie that adds feelings and sensations beyond what the dialogue intends.

It may interest the reader to know that some cultures *only* use nonverbal signals to communicate. For example, certain tribes in Australia

---

5   Beyond Words: An introduction to nonverbal communication, Randall P. Harrison, Prentice Hall, Inc. Englewood Cliffs, New Jersey, 1974, p. 24-25. Harrison mentions one author as listing eighteen different categories of nonverbal behavior. They are a) animal and insect, b) culture, c) environment, d) gestural facial, expression, bodily movement & kinesics, e) human behavior, f) interactive patterns, g) learning, h) machine, i) media, j) mental, k) music, l) Paralinguistic, m) personal grooming, n) physiological, o) pictures, 16. space, p) tactile, q) time.

6   Communication Research Reports, Communication Quarterly, Review of Journals Journal of Social Psychology, Communication Reports, Communication Reports. Psychology Today, Journal of Personality and Social Psychology, Journal of Nonverbal Behavior Nonverbal Communication in Human Interaction, Journal of Applied Psychology of Communication, Educational Psychology, Journal of Psychology, Intercultural Communication: A Reader, Journal of Nonverbal Behavior published in the last quarter of the seventeenth century there were not more than three or four men living who could comprehend it.

7   One of Newton's chief biographers has stated that when the Principia was published in the last quarter of the seventeenth century there were not more than three or four men living who could comprehend it. Another scientist generously stretched the number to ten or a dozen. Even Newton said his book was hard, but he made no apologies. It was Isaac Newton who invented the first satisfactory reflecting telescope. *Five Equations That Changed The World*, Michael Guillen, Hyperion, 114 Fifth Avenue, New York New York, 10011, p 9.

and some Christian monastic orders prohibited speech on religious grounds. The tribes are not allowed to use any verbal messages at all.

This author connects to all the perceived messages, meaning all feelings, ideas, thoughts and silent signals of communication which do NOT connect to verbal speech. A rainbow of seven colors, when compounded becomes white light. That is a nonverbal message to this writer. Harrison explained this in a classroom once and I never forgot it. He said that color was a characteristic of light and the appearance of white light.

Clearly there are nonverbal signals which connect to women and nonverbal signals which connect to men. One book offered the following examples.

Signals performed by females	**Signals performed by males**
Lowers eyes	*Stares*
Smiles	*Frowns*
Tilts head	*Holds head erect*
More positive gesturing	*Less positive gesturing*
Takes up less space	*Takes up more space*
Moves out of his way	*Moves in on her way*
Space/yields space	*Initiates touch*
Accepts touch	*Has erect posture*
Stands/sits with legs together	*Stands/sits with legs apart*
Hands at sides or in lap	*Hands on hips*
Leans into	*Leans over*
Talks more softly	*Talks more loudly*
Less likely to interrupt[8]	*More likely to interrupt*

Some authors describe nonverbal signals in only three areas. Another lists eighteen subjects of nonverbal communication.[9] I believe I have

8   Nonverbal Behavior in Interpersonal Relations, Richmond & McCroskey, Pearson Education, Inc. 75 Arlington St., Suite 300, Boston, MA 02116, p. 233
9   Nonverbal Communications, Randall P. Harrison, Michigan State University Press, 1974, p. 66

culled these down to the most practical ones for business people and interpersonal communication.

Bird watchers may spend an entire day looking for a specific bird they believe is in a certain place; and when they find it they get a flush of joy and excitement, which nobody sees or hears.

My brother has drawn some illustrations for this book. However, his picture will be reveled one page and section at a time.

Try to obtain as much information and meaning as you can from each section of picture you see. You will see only a potion of the total picture on each page. Pictures do have messages. See how accurate you are in each portion.

Notice, you will not get all of the information *until* you see the entire picture.[10]

---

10   MSU Professor. This cartoon was inspired by a classroom demonstration by Professor Harrison at Michigan State University in his classroom where he showed us a similar picture.

SECTIONS OF A DRAWING

From my class as a graduate student at Michigan State University, my professor showed us a portion of a painting and asked us to tell him what we thought we were seeing and what we knew we were seeing. It was amazing how so many of us missed the real message as the painting was revealed one section at a time.

Seeing the whole picture…getting the complete message is as difficult in the language of nonverbal communication as it is in the spoken word or words.

What do you think you know from this picture? How many people do you believe are in this picture? Are the words printed above spoken by one person or two or are these words somebody's thoughts. How do you know that you know this? What else do you know in this picture? Let's look at another section of this picture. On the next page you will see the second portion of the picture. Now what do you know?

So, there are two men and not three. One seems to be dominant. Do you agree?

How would you explain each of these men? What is the item on the right side of the picture?

What else do you think you see?

Let's see more of the picture.

Do you know anything now that you didn't know previously? Is one man more affluent than the other? What is the object on the right? What do you think each man does for a living? How well is each man educated? Or do you have enough information to answer that? Is it possible we make educated guesses by what we see?

Let's look at another section of the picture.

Why is the man on the left hiding a warrant in his left hand? Why is there a police car in the distance? Do you know what the object the man on the right is holding?

Now let's look at the entire picture. Notice how many messages you missed.

Who does the man on the left work for? What is the thing behind these two men? So what is the man on the right trying to avoid? Remember, not everything you see the first time you meet some one will be correct. Take more time in measuring strangers and give more time to knowing them before you make hard and fast opinions about them. A picture is worth a thousand words, but there are many messages in the nonverbal signals. Try to get the correct messages.

The readers will forgive this major 'without-the-body moment.' When I saw the French pantomimist, Marcel Marceau; called by some 'The Professor of art and silence', I was transfixed forever. His body seemed to be boneless. He was so graceful and extraordinarily agile and as someone said, each muscle was almost autonomous and the most expressive face I ever saw. It was a life changing experience to have studied under him in New York City and for a day at The University of Michigan. We eventually traveled to several TV stations together where I, with poor French and Marcel with poor English held several pre-performance interviews.

As a mimist, I performed in this wonderful silent entertainment for years. I never lost my love for the chance to make some one cry or laugh without any words. As a retired mimist, I can still do some of these wonderful mimes.

With Marcel Marceau (left)

THE PHYSICAL NONVERBAL SIGNALS IN ORDER OF VALUE

In subsequent chapters, these nonverbal signals will be examined in more detail.

THE NINE MAJOR NONVERBAL SIGNALS

- Countenance = the feelings seen in the face (Ch 10)
- Gestures = hand movements[11] (Ch 13)
- Expressions = facial signals[12] (Ch 13)
- Silence = its power (Ch 13)
- Eye contact = where the eye looks (Ch 13, 19 & 20)
- Mirroring/Leveling = reflecting other people's signals (Ch 13)
- Listening = the greatest compliment (Ch 13 & 17)
- Tone of voice = a major influence initially (Ch 13)
- Touching = the values and risks (Ch 18)

THE EIGHT SIGNIFICANT NONVERBAL SIGNALS

- Proxemics = the distance between two people (Ch 14)
- Posture = a strong message always (Ch 14)
- Time = it's all over the place (Ch 14)
- Physicality = it also speaks (Ch 14)
- Movement = too little or too much (Ch 14)
- Angle = we're standing almost sideways to a person (Ch 14)
- Dress = an obvious nonverbal message (Ch 14)
- Artifacts = something to think about (Ch 14)

---

11   Nonverbal Communications, Randall P. Harrison, Michigan State University Press, 1974, p. 133
12   How To Read the Language of the Face, M.E. Mitchell, The Macmillan 22A.D. Company, New York, Collier-Macmillan, Ltd., London, 1968, Library of Congress Card Number 68-11429, p. 1-3

THE NONVERBAL SIGNALS YOU CAN TAKE TO THE BANK[13]

- Breath from the mouth
- Covering the mouth
- Down gestures
- Grooming
- Handshakes – five examples
- Index finger messages
- Doubt message

- Confused message
- Surrender message
- Steepling – ego message
- Chin up
- Eye stutter
- Arms crossed
- Sitting messages

For my entire adult life as teacher, professor, speaker, consultant and private nonverbal coaching including and reading many books on the subject, I believe I know what nonverbal signals are as well as any consultant. But, it surprises me at every talk I give, that people have so little understanding of many of these signals.

Fox News with Bill O'Reilly (his show is called "The O'Reilly Factor") has included Ms. Tonya Reiman (a Body Language analyst on his show). Fox News Television has given this subject a major boost with the television public and I am very grateful. For me she seems to get some gestures, but misses others. Her book is titled 'Body Language' and lists five immutable truths about the subject: some I question.

1. Body language is constant.

True, we are communicating signals all the time.

2. Body language is always determined by context.

True, and an excellent point. It depends upon where you give these signals.

3. Body language can never be judged based on one signal.

False. This book list signals you can make a firm judgment on. I agree all other signals require more than one for a clear and true judgment.

4. Body language reveals the discrepancies of what a person says and truly believes.

---

13   Discussed in Chapter 21

Mostly true. However, a chronic liar can look you in the eye and lie very convincingly and it will be nearly impossible to know they are lying.

5. Body language mastery allows you to tune in to micro-expressions; the brief flashes or gestures that betray the inner feelings[14]

True, but few people have mastered this skill..

After lecturing, teaching, doing nonverbal seminars and one-on-one coaching all of my adult life, I have concluded that not everyone finds this subject that interesting. An unscientific summary of my experiences would conclude the following about those who have been exposed to this fascinating subject:

About 10% understand it; use it and make positive changes

About 80 % love it and use it in a modest way

About 10% didn't understand it at all

Some can see nonverbal signals and some cannot. Some people are great communicators and others are not. It is the same for inventors. Why did Newton, Bernoulli, Faraday and Einstein see things that others couldn't see? Just as interpersonal communication skills vary from person to person, so does the ability to read nonverbal signals vary from one to another. Hopefully, this book can improve both groups in a positive way.

AN EXPERIMENT TO DEMONSTRATE OUR DIFFERENCES IN SEEING THESE SIGNALS

Most of us have two eyes, but each eye is focused on two completely different places at the same time. Close your left eye. Now look at an object. Leaving your left eye closed, now bring one of your index fingers into view near that object and hold it still. Remain fixed on that object and without moving your finger, close the left eye and open your right eye. Suddenly your finger has jumped to another position. The brain is empowered to have two eyes focused on different parts of our vision and still focus us on what we believe is one thing.

---

14   The Power of Body Language, Tonya Reiman, Pocket Books, A Division of Simon & Shuster, Inc. 123o Avenues of America, New York, New York, 10020, 2007, p 37-39

Now think about our peripheral vision. Some people have extraordinary side vision; even stronger than straight ahead vision. In the Army this writer was trained for night vision to look slightly left or right of an object we were trying to see and our peripheral vision would see it where our straight vision didn't. Some of us have eyes ruled by our brains to see nonverbal signals and some do not. PERIOD! Maybe we would see these nonverbal signals if we kept one eye closed.

NONVERBAL COMMUNICATION EXPRESSES FEELINGS AND EMOTIONS

Most people, when they hear familiar words or phrases repeated again, will create the same facial expression they made the first time they

heard them. It is extremely likely that when negative subjects come up, our facial expressions will change to our formerly used negative expressions. We do this unconsciously. Contrarily, when we hear words, phrases or subjects we love, our facial expressions look more agreeable and happier and they are almost always the same ones we have used many times before.

When you don't like yourself, a feeling inside your head, you will create negative nonverbal movements and other nonverbal signals, which will eventually communicate various messages of "I don't like myself", "I'm not too happy", "life's not much fun", "I hate such 'n such" or " I don't want to talk about that". The negative signals you gather together may gradually escalate. Your focus on yourself will literately take over your verbal and nonverbal communication. Your negative self image WILL be your main message.

Even if you think negatively, it will create negative body signals. Unconsciously, you will stand differently, gesture differently, have poorer eye contact and give off many signals of a weak self image. A single negative thought, belief or feeling WILL PRODUCE NEGATIVE nonverbal signals and it will do it instantly! All three previous photos are examples. I know many people who have changed their lives by eliminating negative thinking. My grandmother often said, "Ronald, forget yourself!" Think about others. Depending upon your thinking you may look like these nonverbal messages. You can't change some things, but we all need to try to control our feelings and thoughts.

Reiman also claims in her book there are only seven universal emotions or feelings which are claimed by every culture in the world.[15]

They are:

Sadness - Surprise - Fear - Anger

Disgust - Happiness - Contempt

With enormous respect to Reiman, and from my nonverbal experiences, I add a few more universal emotions or feelings. They are:

Despair - Jealousy - Skepticism - Doubt - Arrogance

Humility - Reverence - Humor - Enthusiasm - Submissiveness

Gratitude - Apathy - Complaining - Controlling - Empathy

Regret - Meekness

There may be different cultures on this planet which do not include some of these emotions and feelings, but my feeling is I seriously doubt it.

NONVERBAL SIGNALS ALSO COME IN CLUSTERS: ALL AT ONCE

One spoken word such as the word 'well…' has some meaning, but requires additional spoken words to finish the implied feeling that more words are coming. Even two words such as, 'Yes, but…', or 'I think…' requires more words to communicate a comprehensible verbal statement.

Two nonverbal signals, closing the eyes tightly and compressing the lips tightly may make the listener pause, waiting for more nonverbal signals such as opening the eyes and relaxing the lips. These combined

15   Ibid, p. 44-50

signals are called clusters. A cluster of signals can produce a cluster of spoken words.

The cluster of seven signals in this picture are:

- Head down

- Hand on hip

- One eyelid closed

- One eyebrow up

- Palm up and out

- Mouth twisted

The nonverbal messages for this picture could be: "What?" "You expect me to believe that?" "Are you crazy?" "I don't get it." "That's stupid!" Notice it is usually a cluster of signals rather than one signal.

Basically, all cluster signals here are reinforcing the same message. In the next picture the cluster will include only four of the first previous picture signals. Notice how the nonverbal message differs. This next picture will leave out the signals of the eyelids slightly closed, the twisted mouth and closed eyelid.

Notice how totally different the nonverbal message is now. What do you think this message is saying? Hasn't all of the doubt disappeared? The change in this nonverbal message will have a relationship to the other person's spoken words or their changed expressions. Very subtle changes in the face or hands can make an important difference in a nonverbal message.

Some people inundate us with too many signals in a cluster and, like too many words in a sentence we may see only a few of the signals or hear only a few of the words. People cannot (as a rule) orchestrate their nonverbal signals. They occur spontaneously.

This picture has the following cluster signals:

- Fore finger on cheek
- Thumb holding chin
- Right hand tucked under left elbow
- Head level
- Face calm

What does this cluster of signals say nonverbally? This cluster may mean nothing. It may be a comfort zone for the listener…interested maybe, but certainly what he or she is hearing and seeing doesn't seem to be a problem.

Notice how the nonverbal message changes in the next picture by adding the squinting of the eyes, drawing down the eyebrows and raising one eyebrow slightly; an entirely different nonverbal message.

There are hundreds of very powerful nonverbal messages and hundreds of extremely subtle nonverbal signals. The ability to "communicate a message" without making any sounds from the mouth is extraordinary.

Let's look at some other clusters.

Here is another cluster message. Notice the thumb appears to be holding up the chin; the forefinger is locked on the cheek; the fingers have locked the mouth from speaking. This cluster of signals can mean the listener is bored or not listening or has something else on their mind. When you see these signals, STOP talking and somehow, pleasantly, find out what is going on. By giving them an opportunity to speak they may end the conversation for some reason, which when you discover it, you will be grateful you stopped talking. You then have some control of the situation.

If I saw this cluster of nonverbal signals, I would ask a question such as, "Am I confusing you…or do you have a question or comment?" You may get lucky and find out why they are looking this way. Again, you are controlling the situation and helping them get out of it…for good and purposeful reasons. You win! They still like you; you saw they had something else on their minds and this conversation can happen later. You win!

Here is a picture of a cluster of signals which could be modifying a verbal message. This person doesn't believe what he has just heard spoken, He also might shake his head back and forth; even a very subtle head shaking. Every time you believe you see any signal which may appear as 'doubt' or misunderstanding...**DO NOT PROCEED** until you have cleared up this confusion. It will save you time later. It may save a sale.

After teaching this powerful subject so long, I have learned one absolute point. When you see anything on the face which looks like they didn't get it, or they don't seem to understand, or they seem confused **DO NOT PROCEED. STOP**! As gently as possible, ask if they understood what you have just said. Those who do this have fewer communication problems. If you don't clarify the signals you have just seen, you may give an incorrect message or confuse a person.

When a person didn't understand something and you have continued to talk, they will give you a long series of nonverbal messages such as looking away, looking down, focusing on anything but you. I have seen people shaking their heads slightly back and forth. The message in their head might be, "I don't get this person al all." When they stop talking I will ask a question. Your uninterrupted talking may likely bring about expiration to their initial question. They have forgotten it. You kept talking too long.

This could be that his neck itches. The facial expression will help you. This cluster could mean

"You are being a pain in the neck!"

Here is a closed position usually. Hiding the looking down vulnerable parts of the body with eyes down usually means they have decided to cut you out or turn you off. When you see this cluster, you are not communicating too effectively. Try humor or ask if they have any reactions or comments for you. In other words, try to reconnect.

Here is another seemingly closed position done standing. This time the facial expression is happy and smiling. This closed position becomes a comfortable message.

Remember the crossed arms can be both defensive and comfort. The cluster signal of the face should determine which one. Here the man is smiling, so it is more likely this position is comfort.

When you see this cluster of signals where the person is tightly grip-ping themselves with legs crossed and their head down - plus - an expression that says… they clearly appear to be a very unhappy person …there is a problem. As well as you can, find out if there is a problem.

CHAPTER 5

THE ORIGIN OF NONVERBAL SIGNALS

How and where did humans get their particular nonverbal signals? Were we born with them? Did we get them from our parents, siblings, grandparents or schoolmates? There is research available to suggest much of our personality, likes, dislikes, patterns of speech and a great deal of our behavior was implanted in us when we were in our mother's womb.

NONVERBAL BEHAVIOR IS GENETIC

Research of identical twins separated at birth and reunited years later shows that the similarities of likes and dislikes, clothes, hobbies and nonverbal signals are amazingly similar. Posture and walking styles are often very similar in separated twins.

This writer's interviews with adult twin siblings, who were separated at birth and reunited years later, found that their nonverbal behavior was amazingly similar; their likeness included posture and some gestures. In one interview both acknowledged they had trouble looking people in the eye. Both were insecure and gave few body and face signals.

It is not unreasonable to conclude that nonverbal behavior comes from three sources, genetics, mother's womb and the nurturing of biological or surrogate parents and relatives after birth.

Ms. Reiman also acknowledges that some people have a natural instinct to read 'social clues' or I would say they have an innate ability to read people's nonverbal signals. Ms. Reiman is one who is reasonably good at it. She appears regularly on Fox News' "The O'Reilly Factor" and she (in this author's opinion) is seldom wrong about what she sees;

often she frequently misses or chooses to not mention important signals. In both the Presidential candidate Barak Obama and Bill Clinton interviews she didn't mention, or chose to ignore, extremely important signals given by Obama and Clinton; too important to ignore.

This author believes he has been given this special gift also. I haven't met very many people with this unique gift. So if some people have this gift, did they get it from their parents? Yes. I got it from my father. So, does genetics plays a part. Yes. God gave this gift to my father and I inherited it. I have increased my inheritance by experience, education and years of observing, lecturing and assisting people in their discovery of their good and bad nonverbal messages they are signaling.

VERY YOUNG CHILDREN SEE MORE NONVERBAL SIGNALS

One researcher says very young children are more skilled at reading nonverbal signals than adults, apparently more skilled than they will ever be as adults.[1]

This advantage over adults appears to be during a short period of their young lives; sometimes between 20 to 30 months of age.[2] But it is clear these toddlers frequently can sense something that bothers them and they don't want to be near the person exhibiting those signals.

In my seminars when I discuss this subject about very young children seeing more of these nonverbal signals, I get many stories from parents. One told me that her uncle came to her house to take her child, who was two and a half, to get an ice cream cone, but the child 'did not want to go.' The mother felt embarrassed and insisted her young child go. In a fit of anger the child ran to the other end of the house and wouldn't come back. The parent apologized and the uncle left. I knew how this story was going to end because I had heard this scenario many times before…always about very small children. This woman then said, "My daughter felt something or saw something in her uncle's face which bothered her, but I didn't see." Six years later this uncle was arrested for pedophilia. The research is extensive; very small children (for a

---

1   Inside Intuition, Flora Davis, McGraw-Hill Book Co. 330 W. 42nd St. NY, NY, 1971, p. 151
2   Ibid, p.144-145

few years) see something parents cannot.[3] Child safety experts suggest that if a child does not want to go or be near a particular adult, don't insist; listen carefully to their wishes.

BE CAREFUL!

If, as a parent, you experience this behavior with your child - they don't want to go with a particular adult, DO NOT MAKE ANY HARD AND FAST JUDGMENTS at that moment. You CANNOT correctly conclude anything from your child's refusal to go with someone. There could be many reasonable reasons why the child does not want to go.

The child may have many other focuses such as a video they were watching or they want to return to a toy they were playing with. You cannot make any judgments. But, you can be careful.

Again, don't force your child to go when they don't want to and DON'T JUDGE! It is a signal which, 'could mean'.

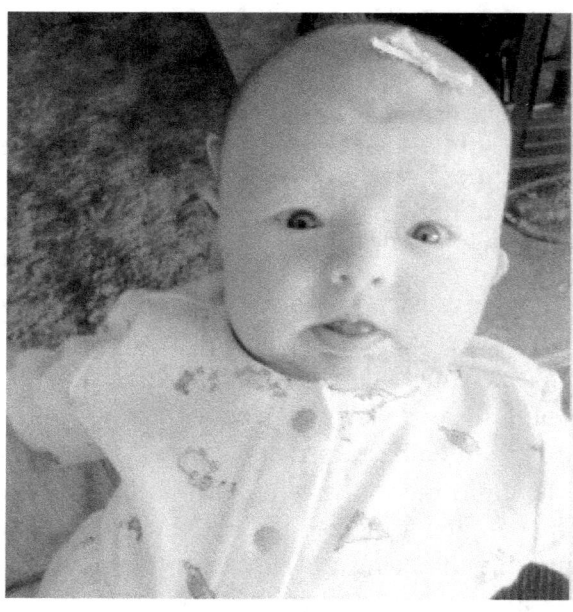

Few facial expressions from a young child are more revealing than worried, scared, or confused. Often, parents ignore these signals. When you see these kinds of expressions, try to find out what may have caused them. Children are normally in a playful mood and unexpected signals may have messages you need to react to. But don't ignore these powerful signals. While adults hide their feelings, children

3   Ibid, p. 152

do not. Pay attention to your children's expressions. Protect them and remember for a few years they can sense things we can't.

My sons often would tell neighbors exactly the way they felt about someone or something and at times it was embarrassing, yet frequently true. Kids grow up fast, so enjoy them each and every day, but protect them. Our children are our most prized possession. And we never own them, but like the treasure of love, we never really remove them from our hearts. When you see a subtle expression of anxiety, it would be wise to discover what may have created this expression.

THE FETUS HEARS SOUNDS AND CONNECTS MOVEMENT TO THOSE SOUNDS AFTER BIRTH

Dr. Henry Truby, Professor of Pediatrics, Linguistics and Anthropology at the University of Miami has done extensive research on the unborn fetus. Ttruby claims that a fetus learns throughout the entire last half of their fetal term.

The fetus becomes very well trained to their mother's voice and possibly the father's also. When this child is born he or she will see expressions and movements which will then be connected to those familiar verbal expressions heard in the womb and the new born will copy these nonverbal signals.[4] This helps stamp certain nonverbal behaviors with those verbal words.

One author writes that as early as a few hours old, babies start to imitate the gestures and mannerisms of their caretakers.[5] She writes it is important to smile at babies and use tender body language with them as you are priming them to respond to others in the same empathetic, bonding way.

She also believes the body language a parent shows a child will invariably be the body language he or she will be attracted to.[6]

THE MUSIC HEARD BY THE FETUS IN THE WOMB MAY WELL LOCK IN AND AFFECT HIS OR HER FUTURE NONVERBAL BEHAVIOR

It is clear that music heard by a fetus in the womb makes a difference in nonverbal behavior. The research is solid. This author sites research which validates that rap music will harm a young child's brain and negatively change their lives and their nonverbal behavior.[7]

---

4   Ibid p. 144
5   Ibid, p. 144
6   Ibid, p. 145
7   "Your Child's Brain" Newsweek Magazine, February 19, 1996, p. 57

Rap music babies grow up desiring and seeking more frantic and exuberant movement. As these children grow they exhibit less interest in standardize schooling.

They are more prone to violence and loud speaking. The study suggests I.Q.s are lower. This study also shows that patient teachers with classical music can make life-long changes in their early behavior.[8] This author adds a personal confirmation. My father played classical music and opera during my mother's pregnancy before I was born. On the day I was brought home from the hospital, my father had to move his 'privately built' automatic record changing player to another room and in the move he broke it. It never worked again.

For me this classical and opera music did not become a standard choice in music again until I was in college. My brother, eighteen months younger never heard any classical music at home growing up. As a teenager, I remember really liking classical and opera music and in my later years it became the only music I listened to. My brother still hates classical music, especially opera. Young kids listening to violent music is harmful.[9]

The research clearly shows that in the last three or four months of prenatal life the fetus has learned many life-long learning skills in the womb, especially music and speech patterns.[10]

Research shows that the fetus which has been moved from an American place to a foreign place is impacted in their speech patterns for life.[11] Research also shows that what the fetus experiences in the womb can influence nonverbal signals. Soon after birth the child will exhibit either an energetic or lackluster behavior, implanted while in the womb. One researcher writes that young children who start speaking earlier (even before two years old) have connected to different sounds and words that their families normally used. The case cited here was research done with American newborns raised in different cultures of language, music and vocal patterns.[12]

---

8 Ibid, p. 145
9 Nonverbal Communication The State of the Art, Harper, Wiens, Matarazzo, A Wiley-International Publication, 1978, p 109
10 Ibid p 146
11 Ibid p 144
12 Ibid p. 145

AN ANGRY FACE IS MORE DEVASTATING TO CHILDREN THAN AN ANGRY VOICE

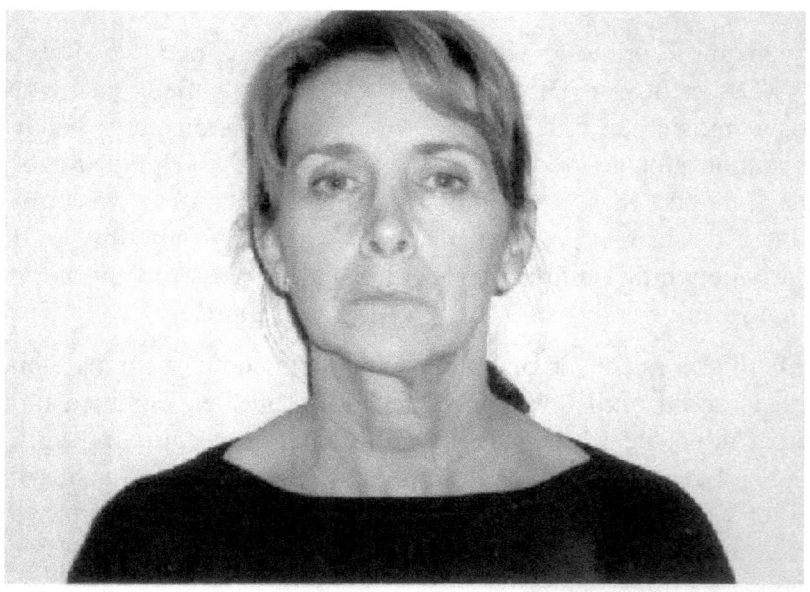

One researcher validates and confirms that nonverbal anger is more disconcerting to a child than angry, loud words. Silva Tomkins writes, "…the prime object of dread in childhood is not an angry-sounding voice, but an angry face."[13]

Research shows that in the last half of a fetus' life in the womb, the fetus can hear their mother's voice. They will hear their mother yelling, hear anger, laughing, singing and other reoccurring verbal expressions.

After they are born and their eyesight is clear, they will then see their mother's face when she repeats these specific sounds.

The very young child will then attach the expression they now see with the sounds which they have heard while in the womb. Thus, the same expression the mother uses when she is yelling, crying, laughing, etc. or laughing will be manifested in the young child at a very early age.[14]

---

13   Inside Intuition, Flora Davis, Signet Book, New American Library, NY, NY 1971, p. 152
14   Ibid p. 153

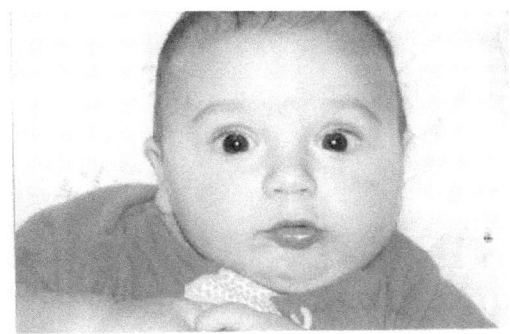

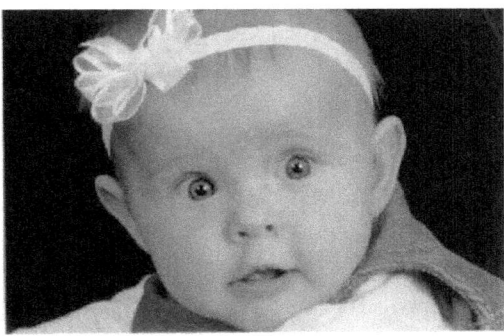

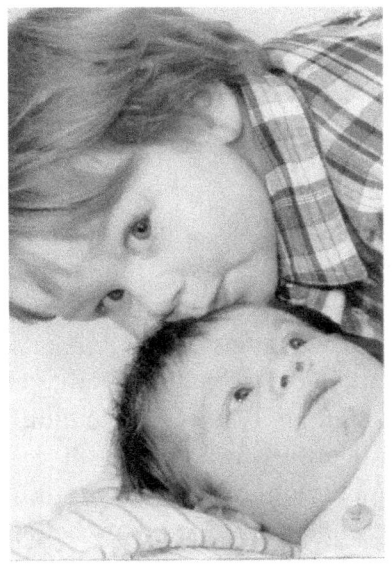

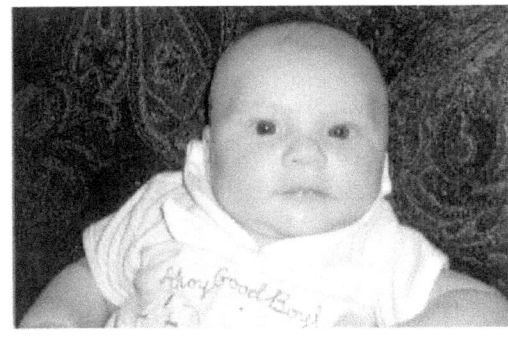

CHAPTER 6

TRADITIONS: THE NONVERBAL IMPLANTS

WHERE MANY OF YOUR NONVERBAL SIGNALS COME FROM

Traditions may be our heaviest, unknown luggage we always carry.

The parents, or as Tolstoy wrote, "those whose task fell on them without choice...describing those human beings who raised the infants (theirs or others) and set their traditions (good, bad and everything in between)."[1] Those parents or parental substitutes molded irrevocable traditions in their children and mainly completed it by ages 8 years of age.[2]

The evidence is beyond question. Traditions implant hundreds of nonverbal behaviors. Think about your own parents or surrogates. Children removed from parents can damage the child forever. Research on monkeys proves this as well.[3]

The famous experiments that psychologist Harry Harlow conducted in the 1950s on maternal deprivation in rhesus monkeys were landmarks not only in primatology, but in the evolving science of attachment and loss. Harlow himself repeatedly compared his experimental subjects to children and press reports universally treated his findings as major statements about love and development in human beings. These monkey 'love' experiments had powerful implications for any and all human separations of mothers and infants, including adoption case studies. In subsequent experiments, Harlow's monkeys proved that "better late than never" was not a slogan applicable to attachment. When Harlow placed his subjects in total isolation for the first eights months of

---

1   The Works of Tolstoi, Vol 1, Black's Readers Services Co.Roslyn, NY, 1928 p.4
2   Ibid p. 4
3   Harlow, Monkey Love Experiments

life, denying them contact with other infants or with either type of surrogate mother, they were permanently damaged. Harlow and his colleagues repeated these experiments, subjecting infant monkeys to varied periods of motherlessness. They concluded that the impact of early
maternal deprivation could be reversed in monkeys only if it had lasted
less than 90 days, and estimated that the equivalent for humans was
six months (this author believes it take less than half that time). After
these critical periods, no amount of exposure to mothers or peers could
alter the monkeys' abnormal behaviors and make up for the emotional
damage that had already occurred. When emotional bonds were first
established was the key to whether they could be established at all.

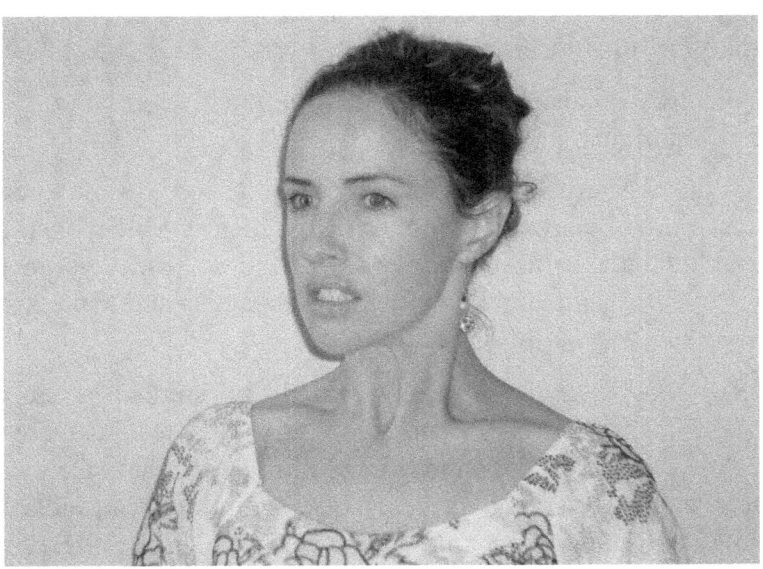

If one or both of your parents were yellers, it is most likely you have
that tradition and you are a yeller also. Tolstoy, in his short story,
"Love" makes a strong case that children do NOT need their biological parents to obtain traditions of behavior. All of us have traditions
or behaviors we can connect to our parents. Even the maternal and
paternal grandparents may have played a major role in the behaviors
we exhibit. Aristotle says we have been molded by succeeding multi-
tudes of generations of family members who preceded us on earth.[4] By

4   Aristotle Poetics, translated by S. H. Butcher, Dover Publications, Inc., Mineola, New York, 1951, p 118. And "Politics, BK. 1 Chs. 8-10 Aristotle Poetics,
translated by S. H. Butcher, Dover Publications, Inc., Mineola, New York, 1951, p
118. And "Politics, BK. 1 Chs. 8-10

eight years old all of us are fairly locked into many of our nonverbal behaviors.

After the age of eight we still learn from those in our immediate families AND from relatives, neighbors, friends, strangers, teachers and many others. All of these behaviors become our traditions. Think about your own childhood, it was then you learned to love or hate, like or dislike, accept or reject, take or give.

It was mainly in these formative years that we were inclined to like or dislike art, books, language, certain music and museums. Some relatives made you laugh and others may have frightened you. By a very young age your traditions were well developed and on a path nearly locked in.

As a nonverbal counselor, I have seen the positive and the negative effects of traditions.

So often the negative experiences turned the person toward a negative direction. Some behaviors are inherited medical problems and affect our behavior later in life. Interestingly, children from dysfunctional families often break destructive learning messages and achieve major successes.

From first-hand knowledge in Hollywood film studios in California and Pinewood Studios in London, England, I have seen many very successful actors, directors and others who came from (their words) completely dysfunctional families. Young children, who lacked loving relationships and had a great deal of rejection early, often become experts at handling rejection and achieve success. Obviously, many struggle for life and are labeled poor achievers.

The most profound impact upon human behavior comes from one of two (sometimes three) people raising them.

In talent auditions for plays and movies, dysfunctional people often get mean rejections from casting directors, many of these people seem to completely ignore these rough rejections, including comments such as "you're awful", "you have no talent" and "get out of the business." Many of these rejected 'actors' achieve great success.

Then there are those whose traditions at home were loving and supportive, but frequently these traditions work in an opposite way in Hollywood arenas. Young people who have had a loving, normal childhood and who haven't been challenged by a lot of rejections in their lives will, in many cases, during casting call rejections, shut down instantly and go back home to their loving parents and safe environment after one rejection.

The Whose Who in the World books are full of famous leaders, scientists, authors, inventors and gifted people who were scarred by horrible traditions including dysfunctional and frightful childhoods. Yet these scarred people achieved major successes.

I grew up with a boy (I'll call Ben) who during the growing years was labeled "a bad boy"; a boy destined for trouble and a boy who probably would quit high school, even end up in prison. Ben had terrible grades throughout most of his schooling and was written off by just about everyone... except his mother. His father would ridicule him in front of me and other boyhood friends.

But, I remember Ben's myopic focus on cars, especially an old, discarded jalopy in his backyard - an old Ford. Ben completely removed the engine of that car and got in a great deal of trouble with his parents for the clutter and individual parts he had left all over his backyard. When we were young most of us would go to the 'old brick yard', an abandoned farm land, which had secret holes and fences that surrounded nothing. We thought it had the biggest trees on earth and most of the neighborhood kids would go there almost every day. Not Ben. He would be in his backyard bent over the battered hood of this old car. His father, out of frustration, decided to get him a part-time job at a nearby gas station where he could help replace oil, clean windshields and whatever else was needed. It was in this gas station that the owner saw what nobody else saw - a boy who was focused on car engines and how they were put together.

The owner taught Ben auto mechanics. He also insisted that Ben finish high school, which he finally did at age twenty. The unbelievable end to this story was that Ben eventually worked for Oldsmobile, a manufacturing plant in our home town.

Later, when I was attending Michigan State University, I ran into Ben on the campus only to learn he was studying engineering on a scholarship he got from the President of the Oldsmobile plant. Ben told me he got the scholarship because he had invented a device which improved the safety of the steering wheel.

The last time I saw Ben was when he was in his fifties. He was working in Detroit for the Corporate Offices of General Motors and was a safety engineer making a great deal of money. Well, so much for poor grades, constant underestimating, and little support from his dad.

Traditions, good and bad can make a lifelong impression on everyone. When Isaac Newton was four years old, he was taken miles from home (an enormous distance in that day) by his mother and given to an uncle he had never seen. His mother was getting married and didn't want him anymore. Two years later, Isaac's uncle died and Newton was placed in a home for orphans. How does one of the world's greatest scientists rise from that childhood shock? Newton must have had special strangers who made constructive influences on him the remainder of his life.

THE GENERATIONAL GOOD JUMPS OF TRADITIONS

Another traditional nonverbal signal for this writer is the similarities between grandsons and grandfathers; the generational jumps of unexpected similarities.

Here is a picture of the author at the age of three. My father on the left was 5 feet 11 inches tall. His father is shown on the right. My grandfather was 6 feet 4 inches tall. I grew to be 6 feet 3 inches. My father was not too involved in the Bible or church. My grandfather carried the Bible and would quote passages almost every day. I became very interested in the Bible and am currently working on a book that deals with nonverbal aspects of the gospel. It's not what we say, but what we do. My grandfather was extremely creative even as an artist fixing metal fenders on banged up Model T's. He was also a painter.

My father never painted one exceptional picture to everybody's memory. Human characteristic traits seem to have nonverbal generational jump.

Here are some other conclusions this consultant has acquired over 40 years. Traditions in families come from parents and grandparents and probably beyond. It would be extremely interesting to see how much of 'us' has come from previous maternal and paternal great-grandparents.

Look at your own family traits and discover how many similarities you have with grandparents. Obviously, we obtain many traditions from our parents also. Traditions create us, even implant us and model us like our families.

Below is a list of behaviors we most certainly got from our parents, grandparents or significant people in our early and formative years. SOME YOU MAY HAVE OBTAINED, OTHERS NOT. I acknowledge that all of these behaviors listed below can be changed, but not very easily.

LIFE LONG IMPLANTED TRADITIONS
Touchers or non touchers
Loud mouths or soft spoken
Strong eye contact or weak
Fear of strangers or fear of nobody
Patient or impatient
Judgmental or not very judgmental
Forgiving or seldom forgiving
Lazy or industrious
Focused or scattered
Ambitious or not
Organized or disorganized
Obsessive or not
Thrifty or not

Secure or insecure
Truthful or a liar
Perfection required or not
Flexible or rigid
Skeptical or accepting
Vain or not
Self abusing or not
Controlling or not
Desire to learn or none
Selfish or selfless
Fashionable or not
A listener or not
A loner or not
Bossy or not
Happy or sad
Reader or not
Talker or less talkative
Joker or serious
Achiever or slacker
Good example or not
A gossiper or not
Dependable or not
Trustworthy or not
Successful or not
Crash proof or not
Religious or not
Opinionated or not
Stubborn or not
Rejection proof or not
Long-suffering or not
Positive or negative

Conclusion: If you have had the opportunity of knowing your parents and grandparents, look for similarities of behavioral and physical similarities. Discover from whom you picked up some of your behavioral traits.

Find out, if possible, where your good jumps came from and also how you got your weak 'trippers' - the behavioral things which you still stumble over.

Often, our traditions are wonderful traits, which we should welcome and be thankful for. Discover your traditional connections to your behavior and your luggage in life should be lighter, your hang-ups and concerns should be more manageable, and life will be more tolerable.

THREE ANECDOTES ON TRADITIONS FROM MY ONE-ON-ONE COACHING

BOB: TRADITIONS WERE WELL INTENDED, BUT TOOK THEIR TOLL

I have known Bob since college days at Michigan State University. When you grow up with someone, it seems you don't notice their poor posture or head down behavior. It was after Bob finished law school when he was seeking a job at various law firms, when Bob called me on the telephone and said, "Ron, can you help me?"

"With what?" I answered.

"I have interviewed at 13 firms. I can't get the second interview."

"Keep going. You have talent and a great brain. You'll get a job."

"I don't think so.

In my nonverbal experience, I have trained myself to listen to the words people say, especially when they have asked for my help. The words, 'I don't think so', may have significance I thought.

Bob and I met a few days later on the same day that another friend of Bob's was coming over to his house also. This friend worked at a law firm in town and was giving Bob some cues to help him get a job at his firm. After introductions, I sat aside and watched their casual meeting. Almost immediately, I saw Bob slump his shoulders down and drop his head while sitting in the chair. When the phone rang Bob got up to answer it and continued his poor posture with head down all the way to the telephone. Was Bob expecting some bad news on the telephone? Why was his posture drastically different and his head bent forward? Shortly, Bob returned from the phone call, still with poor posture and head down. Bob was now less talkative. Why? He hadn't been that way with me at all. Soon, Bob's friend left and we were alone.

Very often when you tell a person about something you saw them doing they will deny it. So I asked Bob if I could mimic his physical behavior I had just seen. I walked to the telephone with slumped shoulders and head down. As expected, Bob denied he did that. I decided I would attempt to find out why Bob had said, those four words I couldn't get out of my head 'I don't think so', when I suggested he would get a job.

From my experience, this kind of body slumping and head down positions is often linked to something and not just an accident. Possibly, as a young boy, he was around someone who had these signals. Maybe it was someone he trusted and inadvertently picked up these signals. I call this phenomenon the traditions of the fathers, meaning what we learn from our parents or relatives when young and impressionable.

As so often is the case, I was correct. Within a few minutes Bob told me what his father had said many times, "You're too tall and this will intimidate girls and even employers. Try to slouch a little or sit down when you can." Bob was 6 feet 10 inches and fairly skinny. His father was almost as tall and was presumably telling his son what he had done.

When I mimic people's body signals, they almost always deny they do them. Bob saw it immediately and knew he was slouching with his head down in every interview he ever took. He was also slouching when he dated girls. His father's well-intended advice had really locked in and it was creating negative nonverbal signals for Bob.

Bob told me he would try to stop copying his father. Not long after this meeting with Bob, I moved to another state and lost contact with him. Several years later, Bob called me to see how things were going. He was now an elected judge in his home town and married to a gal who was a foot shorter. Bob had never forgotten our conversation about walking taller with his head and body up. He also reminded me how difficult it had been to make these changes and now he rarely slouched. He said he has a son who never slouches.

I said that was probably because his son hadn't seen his father do it and he agreed. Good posture pays off. Try it. And if possible, try to discover the traditions you acquired from family members, but don't be angry about any. Our parents got their behaviors from their parents and...so forth.

DON: SOMETIMES OUR NONVERBAL SIGNALS ARE TOO PERFECT AND UNNATURAL (THE HANDSOME MANIKIN WHO COULDN'T SELL)

I heard about Don when I was meeting with Don's boss about his positive and negative nonverbal signals. Don's boss asked if I could fix Don. He told me that Don trained all the salespeople and was an excellent trainer. He said Don knew more about the corporation than anyone. Don was last in sales production.

None of this made any sense. A meeting was set up for me to interview Don. When he walked into the room, I instantly saw what I believed was his problem. Don was one of those who went by the book. Everything he did was to be according to the rules and expectations of others. He wanted to be perfect in following every instruction and seemed too ridged in everything he did. He was dressed immaculately and walked with carefully planned out movements.

Not one strand of hair was out of place. In other words he looked like a handsome, well tailored, living manikin.

It even seemed that Don's greetings to me were well rehearsed. Most important for me was his nonverbal presence. It was too stiff, too perfectly put together, too uncommon. There weren't any flaws in him. He didn't (to this nonverbalist) have any vulnerabilities. He was the too perfect specimen of a sales person. I said to myself, "This guys acts like he can walk on water. No wonder nobody buys from him?"

Probably, not many prospects felt too comfortable around him. BUT… how could I possibly change this 'perfect specimen?'

I was convinced I couldn't. Most changes I accomplish are not traditionalized by parents. He was obviously copying his father and what he learned as a young man was very difficult to change, let alone undo.

Then almost instantly, I had an idea. The following is our dialogue.

"Don, let me see inside your briefcase." This was a very thin case with his embossed initials in gold. I opened it and found almost nothing in it. "Good, give me your car keys." I threw them into the case. I grabbed a cup of pencils and dumped all of them in his case.

"Where's your lunch? Do you bring a lunch?"

"No, I eat at home usually."

"Okay," I answered and grabbed an empty brown bag on a counter in the coffee room. I placed a handful of napkins in the bag and threw it into the case. "Do you wear glasses?"

"Yes."

"Where is the case for your glasses?"

"In my car."

"Go get them."

"What are you doing Ron?"

"I'll show you when you get back." He left and I tried to think of other items I could put into his case. I grabbed part of a newspaper and folded it up and put that in the case. I then added a notebook I was using.

"Here is my glasses case." Don seemed so confused that his formal and stiff presence was now very awkward. My idea seemed to be working.

I put the glasses case into the briefcase which now was pretty well filled.

"Don, you know more about this corporation than any sales person in the company and that might include the president. You teach sales training, so you know the process each sales person needs to follow. BUT, by your own admission you don't close as many prospects as the ones you train. You admit you are last in sales every month.

"I spend too much time with the other sales people."

"I think there is another reason for your poor sales. You're too slick… another word I could use is 'perfect'. You're groomed without a hair out of place.

You present a picture of perfection and your knowledge of the product and company may be over-kill when you are in a sales position.

What followed next was one of my best times in the nonverbal world of helping sales people. "Don, when you get to the next prospect, here is what I want you to do. Make sure your brief case is as full as we have it now and just before you enter your prospect's office, open your case and by using your fingers of your left hand (you need to shake hands with your right) hold this case closed, but not latched, so it won't spill out…yet. Then place it on the table's edge or the prospect's desk…at a corner and make it "accidentally" fall to the floor. The case will empty everything all over the floor.

Then get on your knees immediately, apologizing for this 'accident' and begin to replace all the items which are now on the floor. Your prospect will probably get down and help you fill up your case."

Don looked puzzled. His nonverbal facial signals were almost confused. They were twisted, un-accepting and troubled. He was agitated and kept shaking his head. "I can't do that Ron…that is stupid…I can never do that." He repeated this over and over as I sat without saying a word. Don wanted a reply from me, but I sat silently. After a long pause, I said "You can do this Don…in fact, you have to do it."

Never, I think this is stupid. It's not me.

"Well that's the first statement you've made since we started that is correct. It isn't you, but your 'you' is not working…you're not selling anyone.

It seemed like I spent an hour trying to convince him his first impression in every office was too slick, too perfect and not real. He needed to look vulnerable, like everyone else…with some flaws, some hairs out of place. He even needed to have shoes which looked like they had been worn before instead of right out of the store or off the shoe shine stand.

Don never agreed with my idea or gave any value to my recommendation. He kept saying, "It's not me. I can't do that."

I knew what I was asking was extremely unorthodox, but so was Don's first impressions. I gave up. We shook hands and parted. He didn't say goodbye. My ideas fell on deaf ears I thought. I had failed to persuade him. I began to believe I had crossed the line of positive counsel. The only thing I did was upset Don and probably destroyed any chance of seeing him again.

About four weeks later, Don called me. Here's a summary of the conversation.

"Ron, Don….remember me?" I didn't answer because I didn't remember him. Then he reminded me of my crazy idea of dropping the attaché case.

"Oh…hello…how are you? I'm sorry about our last meeting.

Instantly he said, "Why?"

"You mean you tried it?"

"I did it. There was a long pause.

"Well?"

"It was the hardest thing I have ever done."

"Did it work?"

"We both got on the floor and put the stuff back in. I had showed my wife and small son what you asked me to do. Without my knowledge, my son had added marbles to my case. My prospect and I had more trouble getting the marbles than anything else. Both of us were laughing, almost hysterically. The prospect thought it was really funny."

"Did you make the sale?"

"Yes I did, but…"

"But….? But what?"

"Well,…I got your message. I don't need to do that again."

"So what did you learn about that sale?"

"I gotta loosen up. I have been too stiff and too formal like my Dad. My wife agrees with your ideas. She thinks I should even wear sports clothes too. What do you think of that?" "Pretty radical Don. She knows you better than you do probably. Congratulations."

Don's boss called me a few weeks later and said I was a miracle man to change Don. He said changing Don was harder than changing the Ohio River. Don's boss said he never dropped his case again, but said he did drop his car keys a few times.

The success here was to get Don to see how stiff and unreal all his nonverbal messages were. I was pretty confident his 'stiff and too formal approach' to sales had come from his father, but I had never mentioned it to Don. I had no confidence I could change him. But my idea of dropping the case worked.

People want people selling them to be real and natural…a little imperfect; people like themselves. When we look like people from another planet, they are not as interested as we need them to be. There are many factors in selling a prospect, but one of them is to look like a regular guy with a good product or service and your prospects need to feel comfortable. So drop the ball every once in a while!

HOLLYWOOD: A SURPRISING NONVERBAL SANCTUARY

Hollywood may save more insecure and dysfunctional people there than doctors

The world has places which have special unstated messages. Paris for museums, wine and cheese and cafes. Las Vegas for gambling and spectacular stage shows. Hollywood is the place for movies, movie stars and an atmosphere which beckons the aspiring actor, screenwriter and animator. As television and film has been a great part of my life, I suggest Hollywood also has an enormous 'without the body' nonverbal message.

Just about everyone I know has a dream. Everyone has a hope and an ambition to do something bigger than themselves, even bigger than their parents.

And these dreams are also in people who are insecure or extremely insecure. They include people who have learning disabilities, perceived or actual. Insecurity STOPS many people from trying.

How many young people do you know who you believe may have had a difficult time in their adult life? You believe this because they have had some difficult times and mainly 'failed' at everything they tried as a young person. Regrettably, many young people have learning disabilities. So often, these people have been told 'NO' so many times by their parents, teachers, friends and relatives, they don't hear it any more.

Yet there still exists in some of these people, the belief that they 'can' achieve something in their lives. Granted, not all of them believe that.

Today, we have many people who are labeled as having dyslexia, ADD (attention deficit disorder), hyperkinesias et al and most people would say these behaviors are negative symptoms which require medical help. Some families and teachers inadvertently make wrong judgments about these 'handicapped' people. There appears to be some evidence that people with ADD and dyslexia have talents and skills far exceeding those who appear more healthy and 'normal'. Then there are people who are born blind or deaf who accomplish great things. The fact remains. Many people whose family and friends 'write off' succeed extremely well. Here's an overview of several people identified with those dreaded "you'll never make it" disabilities.

• *Isaac Newton* was given away by his mother to an uncle he never knew when he was only four years old. Then his uncle died and Newton ended up in an orphanage at six years of age. Rejection at this age usually has life long negative ramifications.

• *George Washington* not only was elected by the Electoral College by the only unanimous vote for our President in our history, but may have been one of our least educated. His schooling was brief and narrow. As an adult one observer wrote, "When I first became acquainted with the General, his writing was defective in grammar and spelling, yet a man who always sought truth and righteousness, a man without selfish motives in every sense of the word, a wise, a good and a great man." When he died Jefferson wrote, "...verily a great man has fallen this day in Israel."

• *Beethoven* wrote his 9th Symphony when he was totally deaf.

• *Thomas Paine,* an Englishman living in London, who we first meet in history when he is thirty-seven years old and who had lived all of those years in personal failure. He failed as a tax collector and he failed at teaching twice. Then he met Benjamin Franklin in London and his life (and America's) changed forever. With letters of recommendation from Franklin, he sailed for Philadelphia and was hired by a printer. He soon became an editor for a city magazine. Since Paine hated monarchies everywhere, he decided to write "Common Sense", the most eloquent reasoning for separation of the Colonies from England. It was a major hit and sold widely in England and America. It would have equaled over 10 million copies today. It was the engine that sped up the idea of independence. In one brilliant stroke, Thomas Paine gave no speeches, but spent his time silently without verbal comments and connected liberty with rebellion and did more for America's independence from England than all the armies of Europe that came to America's aid during the Revolutionary War.

• *Helen Keller* became deaf and blind at 19 months of age, yet graduated from college and traveled the world as a speaker and author.

• ***Thomas Edison*** couldn't read until he was 12 years old and failure was his modus operandi. After 1,000 failures trying to invent the light bulb, his assistant was ready to quit. Edison had more failures in him. After his 3,000th failure his team invented the light bulb.

• ***Albert Einstein*** didn't talk until he was three. He had difficulty doing math in school and could barely express himself.

• ***John Milton*** wrote Paradise Lost when he was blind at age 42.

• ***Abraham Lincoln*** suffered from sever depression and twice people had to watch over him for his own protection.

• ***Jay Leno*** had such bad grades he couldn't get into any college. He selected a college close to his boyhood home which had rejected him many times. He sat in the college's Admission Office twelve hours a day, five days a week until they let him in.

• ***Michael Faraday*** rarely attended school. His schooling had gone from bad to worse, while he lived on nothing more than several loaves of bread a week. At 13 years he could barely read or write. Yet, he is considered one of the five greatest men of science, discovering the law of electromagnetic induction, which ultimately led to the discovery of electricity.

• ***Alexander Graham Bell*** had a major learning disability, which some people today have labeled dyslexia.

CHAPTER 7

DO NONVERBAL SIGNALS HAVE AN EXACT MEANING?

Some do. Most do not! Too many body language experts say that a certain nonverbal signal has an exact meaning every time. In the hundreds of non-cluster signals seen by this author, there are ABOUT a dozen nonverbal signals which, unequivocally, have the exact meaning every time they are seen. I know of a few signals which frequently do have an exact meaning. However, the 'may mean' out numbers the 'do mean' by a gigantic percentage. The point of this book is to make you aware that these signals 'may mean'. This is a valuable tool in effective communication. Whether they exactly mean is irrelevant. It's extremely helpful to know theses 'may mean' signals.

All of the other hundreds of single or cluster signals 'may' have a meaning you can depend upon. Rubbing the nose can mean you are thinking 'no'. Rubbing the nose could also mean your nose itches. When you see this 'rubbing the nose' signal, it provides you important information. Is the person thinking 'no' or does their nose itch?

Understanding nonverbal signals correctly gives you communication power.

When you see a signal or cluster of signals, which (to you) seems incongruent to the verbal message, STOP and politely ask if your verbal message was understood. Find out (at that moment, if possible) are you both, on the same page in comprehension and clarity. This is why nonverbal messages can become a powerful tool in communication; it reduces vagueness, incorrect meanings, assumptions and poor interpersonal communication skills. In other words, recognizing these nonverbal signals offers you communication power.

Not all nonverbalists and body language 'experts' agree that nonverbal signals 'may have an exact meaning. Too many make conclusive statements such as "every signal always means" and that's when they get off track.

A good example for this author was when the Fox News' body language expert was at the end of her segment. There was no more time. Bill O'Reilly had said "thanks and see you next week" when she quickly interrupted to remind Mr. O'Reilly she had a 'disclaimer' she needed to squeeze in. It clearly showed that this expert, who had mentioned many body language signals before, all with conclusive meanings now wanted to clarify those statements. She had always said, this signal means such and such every time you see it. It was only a matter of time when a viewer would have taken issue with that statement. So, Bill then said to her, "Quickly, I'm out of time." She then gave a shocking and very short statement. "Body language signals aren't true." I couldn't believe it. An amazing and incorrect statement for an expert who had claimed many times these body language signals were always true. What I believe she was trying to say, but never really did, "Sometimes these body language signals are not always true."

This nonverbal writer believes there are very few signals you can take to the bank every time you see them, but there are some listed in Chapter 21 that we will explore in detail..

CHAPTER 8

AN EXERCISE TO OPEN YOUR EYES

In the following column, write down the seven things you like about your first time prospects or opposing negotiator, or manager/leader, or fiancée, new girl/boy friend.

1. _____

2. _____

3. _____

4. _____

5. _____

6. _____

7. _____

Now place these things in column A if the things you like are mainly nonverbal. Place those things you like in column B if they are mainly verbal.

A. NONVERBAL	B. VERBAL
_____	_____
_____	_____
_____	_____
_____	_____
_____	_____
_____	_____

Notice that the things you liked about your first time encounters are mainly _____. Remember this as you move through the book.

CHAPTER 9

THE WORLD STAGE
FOR NONVERBAL EVENTS

SEPTEMBER 11, 2001

Prior to 9/11 New York City was a place where people hid their expressions for safety and privacy. On public transportation people had the frozen look, indifference, or a false grin. Having lived in New York City for three years, this kind of behavior was common and done out of self preservation and most of it was well meaning. Then 9/11 changed the city in a monumental way. The cool gaze melted. Pretentiousness faltered and New Yorkers embraced a suffering situation. Non-touchers were now hugging strangers. People who had no eye contact before were now looking into everyone's eyes with compassion and tenderness.

Isolated recluses in New York City were now bonding with total strangers in conversation, touching, assisting; even taking dust covered strangers into their private apartments. Everyone was helping and worrying about everyone else. Strangers serving strangers was the major task of those horrible weeks. 9/11 transformed New York City and a nation.

People who had spent every hour of their lives in that city hiding and guarding their privacy were now available, open, and as some have written, emotionally nude; crying in front of strangers, holding anyone who needed holding.

STRANGERS HELPING STRANGERS

Cell phone calls, which had been extremely private prior to 9/11, were now made in front of groups of strangers on street corners while they were crying. Nothing was private for those weeks. No one was a stranger for those weeks.

Anthropologists, psychiatrists, sociologists and nonverbalists sped to the city to study these amazing changes. One question they wanted answered was how long would this new behavior last. It appears that these new and different nonverbal behaviors lasted approximately three months and subsequently, the old attitudes returned.

Unusual and new nonverbal behavior can be instigated by events such as 9/11 and almost always this new and changed behavior slowly returns to previous behavior.

These messages and signals which can be seen, but many are not seen. Some unspoken signals can create major disasters.[1]

HURRICANE KATRINA: ANOTHER NONVERBAL EVENT WITHOUT-THE-BODY (WTB)

There are many nonverbal messages which are communicated without any human body. Christ for example, at the setting of Caesarea Philippi, was standing probably facing away from, but in front of several niches cut out of a mountain wall. Here were displayed several pagan gods, which all the disciples could easily see in the background. It is here that Christ asked Peter, "Whom do men say that I am?" And Peter answers, "Thou art the Christ." KJV Mark 8:27 Standing in front of that wall of pagan gods makes Christ's question much more powerful.

1   Five silent mechanical sequences occurred during the Three Mile Nuclear plant meltdown and had these five sequences happened all at once, a major disaster would have occurred. From the book *Normal Accidents*.

A sunset, cloud formation, a beautiful garden, a picture of an appetizing sandwich, all have wonderful messages and no human body was part of this message. This author believes there are more WTB nonverbal messages than the messages with the body.

Katrina was another WTB nonverbal event. Only this time most people were isolated; cell phones were dead; deep water and dangerous currents kept people alone on rooftops and in attics where some were eventually discovered dead. Many stood alone in six feet of water with no one near them for hours, hoping to be spotted by helicopters already full of occupants. The same nonverbal issues in New York City repeated themselves in New Orleans. As in New York City...when the event became yesterday's news, the residence of these cities returned to their guarded selves, but neither residents of these two cities would ever be the same. Both cities were major axial or pivotal events and major changes in our societies. These are explained in my book,

A family crisis such as a home being destroyed by fire will change behavior; touching will increase, eye contact will be stronger, feelings

will be softer and tone of voice will usually soften. Again, these non-verbal changes don't last long for most of the victims.

Soon the non-touchers are not touching any more. Relatives, who were not too close and who became extremely close for awhile, soon returned to their previous behavior. In a crisis, most of us turn to more loving, caring, touching, sharing, serving, but traditions and real emotional hang-ups keep some of us from using these great attributes on a consistent basis.

An automobile accident can change the lives of many people in a second. But the nonverbal behaviors, which changed for a period of time because of the accident, will soon return to their previous ways. One man who lost two sons in a car accident told me, "I really cared for my grieving wife and became a toucher for a few weeks, then I returned to my old and more comfortable non-touching ways. And it was difficult…the more touching I tried to do."

He and his wife grew apart very quickly and divorced within seven months after their son's death. He hasn't spoken to his ex-wife since. He also said his non-touching behavior is even worse than before his divorce. Similar stories I have heard too often.

About a year later he telephoned me to announce he was getting remarried. I started to ask if he was marrying a non-toucher when he interrupted me and said, "…and she's like me about not touching, hardly at all. What do you think of that?" I thought it was sad, but remained quiet. He then said, "But I think we would be better off touching a little bit more." Before I responded, he said, "I know you think I should, but it's really hard."

Non-touchers would rather do just about anything except being more of a toucher. Those who are non-touchers reading this, it is true that this writer has a firm belief that touchers are healthier and, for most, happier, but it is extremely difficult to change this behavior overnight. Most decide not to.

From this consultant's experience, I believe the following facial expressions most likely reveal people who are NOT likely to be classified as touchers, but are those of a non-toucher.

CHAPTER 10

COUNTENANCE...
YOUR TRUE MESSAGE BOX

FACIAL EXPRESSIONS SHOULD ALSO
BE CALLED COUNTENANCE

Every nonverbalist writes about facial expressions as being one of the most important.[1] I agree, but I also call it countenance, because it includes more than the movements of the mouth and eyebrows. Countenance is the look on a person's face -their feelings expressed by that look. Countenance is normally not understood by most people. One of my favorite ministers often talked about countenance being either bright or dark. The feelings of good, friendly, caring and loving and their opposite feelings can be seen (by some people) in people's countenances. Drug addicts have a darker countenance than a bridegroom at a wedding; not because an illegal drug addict is mean and ugly, but because the illegal drug addict suffers from pain, illegal behavior and the enormous efforts to hide their addiction. All of these feelings will produce a darker countenance.

OUR FACE IS OUR MESSAGE BOX

Our face is our main 'message box' of expressions, emotions and feelings. Our face can silently shout a message of fear, joy, anger, doubt or love and it can happen as fast as turning on a light bulb or turning a light off. Very few people can control these silent signals of feeling. Contrarily, as the saying goes, some of us wear our feelings on our face all the time.[2] Remember, "The light of the body is the eye." Luke 11:34

---

1   Over 1,000 different expressions are possible. Inside Intuition, Flora Davis, McGraw-Hill Book Co. 330 W. 42nd St. NY, NY, 1971 p. 45

2   "Learning is acquired by reading books, but much more necessary learning, the knowledge of the world, is only to be acquired by reading people and studying all the various editions of them." Lord Chesterfield, "Letters to His Son"

There are also some people who deliberately try to hide all of their emotions, even though some people can see their attempt to mask them. Masking of one's feelings also produces a particular signal in the face and some can even see that message. I have seen it and I have heard people say, 'No', but I could see they didn't mean it. It seems we learn to mask our feelings very early in life.

FACE READING IN SECTIONS

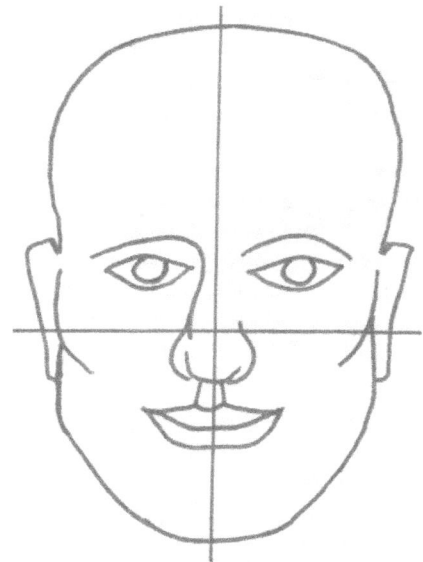

Harrison reminds us that 'Face Reading" was an ancient and venerable art, comparable to reading tea leaves, the palm, or the bumps on the head. A legend in the Talmud tells of 'the science of physiognomy ' in the time of Moses.[3]

According to the story, a famous king sent his court painter to capture the likeness of Moses so that his wise men could analyze this famous face so the king would know what made Moses so great. The king could then cultivate these qualities in himself. But when the painter returned with the likeness, the king was outraged. The painting represented the worse possible set of characteristics that could be collected

3   Physiologists have estimated that the human facial musculature is such that over twenty thousand different facial expressions are somatically possible. To date, they believe they have isolated twenty-two kinemes in the face and head area. Nonverbal Communication: The State Of The Art, Harper, Wiens, Matarazzo, John Wiley & Sons, New York, 1978, p. 123

in one man's face; each feature reveled conflicting and terrible flaws of character.

Another interesting face book is *How To Read the Language of the Face*, by M.E. Mitchell.[4]

Dr. Leopold Bellak wrote 'Reading Faces' (1981). I highly recommend this book as it teaches us that depending upon which eye you select to look at, the message you seem to get from one eye will be different from the other.

Try it. It works. Try it now with a real human face. Each section of the face will be shown separately.

FIRST TIME MEETING...
THE EYE SELECTION MAKES A DIFFERENCE

Every photograph of a face which has been divided into four sections and shown to my seminar clients has always produced at least two different messages or feelings (sometimes three or four) about the person they are looking at.

It confirms what Dr. Bellak has demonstrated. Each eye has its own message. Even each side of the mouth has a different message.

Often, when I look at a person's left eye and it seems to create an uncomfortable impression, I will move my eye to their other eye. It is amazing to me how a first-time meeting changes in our feelings.

So it is true...some people's faces have a 'best eye' to look at.

Now, on the following page is a photograph which has been sectioned in four pieces. Look at the left eye and one half of the nose. While looking at this section make a note how you feel, what impression you have from this portion of the face.

Then look at the picture of the right eye.

What is the message you get from the first and second pictures of the eye? Notice that these messages may have changed. Then look at the mouth; first the left side then the right. See the face as it is divided into different sections and how each communicates; perhaps differently.

---

4   The Macmillan Company, New York, Collier-Macmillan, Ltd., London, 1968, Library of Congress Card Number 68-11429

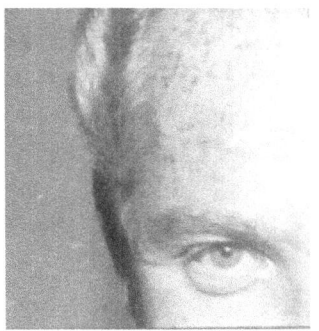

Congratulations, you have just read a face. Now try to repeat this while looking at a live human being during a first-time introduction.

From my experience, every face has a best side or section. So what did we learn? There will be a mixture of character traits such as sadness, anxiety, fear, joy or happiness in every face. Some people will make quick, initial decisions about one section of the face they accidentally focused upon. This quick decision could easily have become a lifetime mistake about that person. This Reading Faces can be done, but it takes some practice to do it well.[5] For more information on this fascinating subject, you might want to obtain, the book by Dr. Bellak.[6]

Everyone has seen a face for the first time which they like immediately. The face looks friendly, even loveable. Their face reveals many good impressions and everyone wants to get to know this person. There is goodness in the face. I also know that these great countenances come from kind and good examples, most often good parents. Again, some people reading this will know exactly what I am talking about. Others will not.

So countenance is the best word for our facial expressions and embodies greater and more meaningful messages. Ms. Reiman calls the face the "Billboard to the soul."[7] The following statement is my belief

---

5   Ibid, p. 116
6   Reading Faces, by Dr. Leopold Bellak and Samm Sinclair. It is a quick read and validates the process. The ISBN number is ISBN 0-03-057869-8
7   The Power of Body Language, Tonya Reiman, Pocket Books, A Division of Simon & Shuster, Inc. 123o Avenues of America, New York, New York, 10020, 2007, p 43

based upon a lifetime of studying and counseling hundreds of nonverbal clients.

Soon after birth a person's countenance is molded by their parents and siblings. In my opinion, by the age of eight the child's countenance is set for life. This countenance can be negatively altered (even for life) by an extremely traumatic event or abuse. But excluding these traumatic experiences, their countenance is locked-in forever.

WHAT YOU THINK AND DO CONTROLS YOUR COUNTENANCE

A person's countenance is controlled by what they think…and by what they do. A person's countenance (face message) can change in a fraction of a second. So when someone says a word which jars or shocks you or pleases you, your face can change in less than a second. This change has little muscle feeling to make you realize you have instantly changed your facial expression, but nearly everyone (not all) will see this change. Therefore, think positive thoughts instantly, especially when an unpleasant word or phrase is heard…and very likely your face won't change. Wouldn't you feel better if the person you are talking to doesn't 'see' your face of pain, anger or other negative expressions which they caused. It is most likely, they won't understand or may misunderstand you new expression.

Countenance can be seen by some people and to those who can see it, they will see a brightness or a darkness and every shade; a light or darkness.

WE CAN CONTROL OUR COUNTENANCE

We can control our thinking and feelings by using positive thoughts. William Buckley, a former successful author and Public Television talk-show host was almost always smiling while he was interviewing guests on his show.

That includes people he disliked vehemently. How did he do this? He was consciously controlling his face, appearance or countenance by thinking some kind of positive thought...forcing his familiar smile... which never looked forced. Once, I had the opportunity to be on his television studio set during one of his taped interviews. Everyone clearly knew he and his guest did not agree on much and did not like each other.

Following the taping of the show, I had an opportunity to ask him, "Mr. Buckley, everyone knows you two gentlemen don't agree on much and even dislike each other, but during your entire interview, you never stopped smiling." His response was, "Oh...did you notice?" He confirmed that he did this, but after so many years interviewing guests, he probably did it now because of habit. Positive changes, will, if sustained long enough, become good habits. Try it!

Conflicts, disagreements or unrepentant 'bumps' may suddenly occur in a marriage or in parenting moments, or selling or negotiating. Immediately, think positive thoughts about the person you are in front of and your countenance will nearly always look positive.

If you don't like your spouse at that moment or a prospect or adversary in negotiations, something in your countenance will noticeably change and possibly darken or be slightly distorted and will produce negative nonverbal signals…and they will see them! And all of these changes will happen unconsciously and extremely fast.

This author has learned to successfully control his countenance instantly when hearing a stupid, senseless or harmful word or sentence. I acknowledge it takes practice, but has many rewards. Remember, in every criticism there is some truth and that truth is rarely discovered at the moment you hear the criticism. A famous quotation reads, "Trust not a man's words, but his countenance."

The best countenances I see are most often in young children. Many people call it 'innocence.' Here are some photos which show excellent countenances.

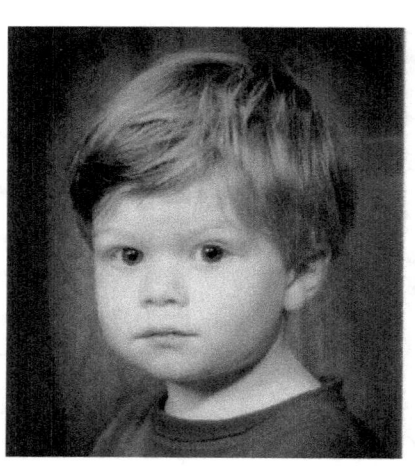

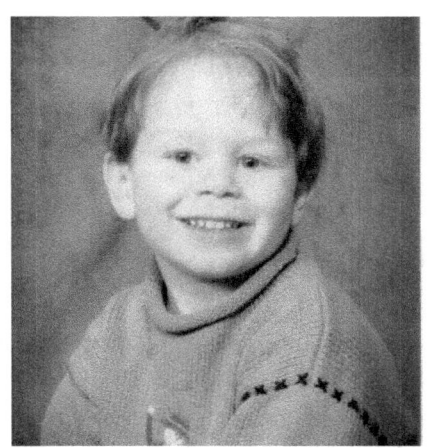

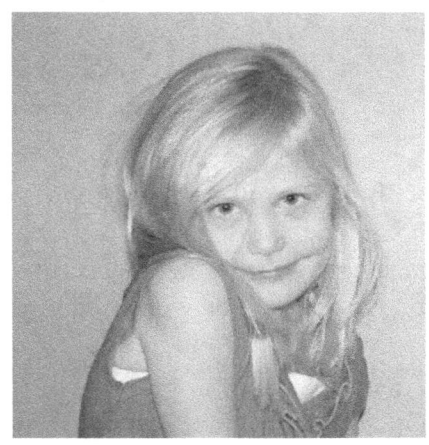

TWO COUNTENANCE ANECDOTES FROM MY ONE-ON-ONE COACHING

JUNE AND LEWIS: *HER COUNTENANCE SPOKE LOUDER THAN HER VOICE...SOME PEOPLE JUST CAN'T HIDE THEIR NONVERBAL FEELINGS*

June was a very pretty girl with a great smile, but everyone knew when she was either unhappy, angry or in a bad mood. Unconsciously, her face screamed these kinds of messages of her inner feelings. If someone said something she didn't agree with, her face told you so immediately. She absolutely could not hide her feelings.

I worked with June as a consultant for about three days. Our plan was to try to say things which would trigger every emotion possible WITH-OUT her face revealing her emotions. It didn't work. June simply could not hide any feelings. Some of her feelings had a distorted look. If she doubted what you were saying even a child could see doubt in her face. This caused a significant problem in her marriage.

About three months after I had left this city, I had another person (Lewis) very much like June, whose feelings were always known by everybody. He was a salesperson and often he would get a comment from a prospect which would make him angry and nearly every time the prospect would either apologize or a couple of times they would end the sales call. Lewis wanted my help more for his marriage than his sales position. I have deliberately avoided marriage counseling for many reasons. Not the least is I have not been trained in the area.

Lewis did not care. He and his wife had seen marriage counselors often with zero results. Lewis thought I could help him. I said I doubted I could do anything more than a marriage counselor could. Before Lewis left our second meeting, I asked him about his mom and dad. He told me his father was worse than he was. His feelings were a neon sign to everybody.

His father had a difficult time with employers and had changed jobs so often everybody had lost count. Lewis agreed his problem had been imprinted on him by his father. He knew that, but knowing that only made it worse.

We talked about some nonverbal signals and I left town feeling badly that I had not been able to help either June or Lewis. I had a long drive to my next nonverbal talk and was replaying my conversations with June and Lewis over and over in my mind when suddenly I remembered what my father had said one afternoon when he was driving me to an airport. Let me first set the scene before I reveal what my father said.

Before joining a Michigan television station, I had worked with The Jackie Gleason Show (CBS, New York City) and had appeared on Kraft Television Theater (NBC) several times in non-speaking parts. The director of Kraft thought I could be a network television director and advised me to return to Michigan and get a bachelor's Degree in Television Broadcasting and come back to New York and he would help me get that job.

Because of the New York experience the local television station in Lansing hired me as a director. This meant I had been hired over several men in line for that director's job. That made one man very angry and he began to do whatever he could to get me fired. He spread false stories that most didn't believe, but eventually they got the attention of the 'Old Man', owner and president of the television station. I got the pink slip with the Old Man's scribbled initials on it. That always meant 'you're fired'

When I got home that night I told my father. He said, "Is your boss correct? Are you guilty of something?" I said no. Then he gave me some advice I never forgot and walked away. He said, "If you're not guilty, forget about it and forgive the man who spread the rumors. That will change your face." Change my face? What did that mean I thought. My Dad talked about admitting if I was wrong, but just as wrong was not forgiving the man who tried to get me fired. That seemed impossible. I didn't like this guy.

I've learned forgiving sets you free and your face will seem brighter. That is good countenance. My father had said, If you are not guilty your face should show that. Faces don't lie unless you have learned how to lie. He was talking about countenance, but I had no idea about that at that age. I never forgot that conversation. It stayed in my brain and when I started my nonverbal career, I used it many times when talking about countenance.

I decided to tell both Lewis and June my father's advice. I could not reach Lewis, but did talk to June. I gave her my father's advice. She said thanks and we ended the telephone call.

I didn't hear from June until I was in Lexington, Kentucky five years later. I had been advertised as a speaker for the Lexington Board of Realtors and she heard about it and attended. It was after my talk when she surprised me.

The Director of the Board was scheduling all my counseling sessions. I asked June to talk to the Director so we could get together. I told June I was looking forward to it. She said, "I don't need to talk to you. You already talked to me." I was briefly dismayed with the comment. Seconds later, June said, "It's working."

"What's working?" I asked. She answered, "Your comment to forgive myself." Before I could comment, June said, "I know you told me to forgive my dad, but I think I needed to forgive myself for the bad feelings I had toward my dad. My dad and I are closer than ever because I forgave him for all that stuff...." June was obviously a happier person. Her countenance was brighter and she really seemed content with herself. I told her she looked great and was happy to see her, but especially happy that she and her dad were closer. She didn't come to my counseling class in Lexington and I never saw her again, but, as it has happened so many times in my life, no payment could equal the pleasure June's comments had been to me. Money can't buy those kind of rewards. Correcting bad feelings 'will' change your countenance.

REGGIE: *IN NO MAN'S LAND OF ALASKA*

While training a salesman in Alaska (I will call him Reggie), I had the chance to visit many homes in and around Wasilla. One of the homes we visited was deep in the woods, down a long, winding, dark and narrow road. When we arrived at the house it was night time. We were greeted by the client, an 18-year-old young man.

The salesperson was in the middle of his presentation when suddenly the front door was flung open nosily. We were alarmed to see a man standing there pointing a pistol in our direction. The man was the boy's father. He yelled, "Is everything okay boy?" The 'boy' quickly calmed his father down and he placed the pistol in his jacket pocket. Within seconds the father was out of the room and apparently in the kitchen. The salesperson was supposed to show his company's product and services to the parents, but this dad was not interested.

I concluded immediately this sales call was a waste of time and signaled the trainee to end the meeting. As we were getting up, the father came into the room and asked why we were talking to his son. It was then that I really saw the boy's father. This man's countenance was dark...very dark. In fact, from my experience of seeing countenances of good, bad, and everything in between, clearly this father was evil.

I was anxious to leave, but the father kept asking questions. Besides a bad countenance, I saw a signal that seemed odd. The father kept his left hand in his jacket pocket. To see some of the salesperson's literature, the father needed to turn some of the pages which he chose not to do. It seemed to me that he didn't want to take his left hand out of his pocket. That signal didn't make any sense, but it was a solid signal. I decided to dismiss it.

Within a couple of minutes we were told by the father that he had all the information he needed and said, "My son will call you if he's interested." We were out the door and I was glad to be gone.

The next morning Reggie and I were having breakfast in a Wasilla restaurant. At the counter were two deputy sheriffs. They were talking to the waitress about a robbery which took place the night before. One of the statements I heard was, "…well this guy's hand is either broken or in bad shape." I then remembered the two signals I saw the previous night. I decided to talk to these two deputies.

I told them that I was a nonverbalist and was with a man who seemed to be hiding his left hand. These deputies didn't understand anything I said and especially about being a nonverbalist. They gave me a weak 'thanks' and went back to their meal. I went back to my table and told the sales trainee what I had just done. The sales trainee knew about my expertise and also knew the two deputies sitting at the counter. He went over and said they should check the man out we visited last night. That got them very interested, but not in the man. They wanted to know more about me.

The deputies came to our table and wanted to know who I was and what I did, rather than what I saw last night. My explanation didn't seem to satisfy them. One deputy was doubtful, but the other was possibly interested. I didn't think they were interested at all. They soon left and I forgot all about it.

A few days later I got a call from this sales trainee and he told me these deputies had gone to the home where the man with the dark countenance lived and after a brief investigation solved the robbery. P.S. The man's fingers had been broken when the victim slammed a door on them.

When I see a dark countenance, I sometimes look for other signals. Dark countenances are strong messages for those who can see them. Dark countenances almost every time signal bad behavior!

CHAPTER 11

POSITIVE & NEGATIVE NONVERBAL SIGNALS

Everyone receives and elicits nonverbal signals. Everyone also has some signals which are, on a first meeting of another person, either neutral (little to no impact), negative or positive and can produce a variety of silent messages such as:

I don't believe you.	I don't trust you.	I didn't hear you.
I didn't understand you.	I am not interested.	I agree.
I think that's stupid.	I really like you.	I believe you.

We produce many nonverbal messages while meeting another person for the first time. These messages are given by our tone of voice, our head position, eyes, face, body, clothes, posture and even by our physicality (skinny, fat or weak looking or muscle bound).

More people than I can count have asked me for my analysis of their 'negative' nonverbal signals to help them eliminate them. It is interesting that almost no one asks me about their positive nonverbal signals. When counseling, I have treaded lightly on my responses when I am asked about their negative signals, as I realize quickly whether they are 'teachable' or not and if they can handle any answer I give which is one they are not aware of.

Knowing that people give signals, which can create bumps in your verbal communication, is very valuable and I look forward to this opportunity every time. I humbly say I have helped many people improve their employment opportunities, spousal relationship, negotiation and hiring skills. To my knowledge (no one ever indicated it) I haven't hurt anyone.

For those who cannot attend my seminar, ask people you really like if you have characteristics or body messages which aren't positive. It's a start and knowing our short comings in face-to-face communication can help us, especially being a wife, mother/father or employee.

The nonverbal signals mentioned in this book should be a start for you and let me state, all of the signals mentioned in this book relate exclusively to our culture. It is true that many nonverbal signals of Americans have the same or similar meanings as many Eastern nations, but the exceptions are too great to include in this book. Let's now look at the Major Nonverbal Signals.

CHAPTER 12

THE NONVERBAL SIGNALS

Two Categories

How many nonverbal signals are there? For this author, every nonverbal signal can be listed under just three categories listed below. This book will focus *only* on 13 of these signals listed separately in two categories.

- The Eight **Major** Nonverbal Signals
- The Eight **Significant** Nonverbal Signals

We will begin our focus on the Eight Major Signals in the next chapter. These you will see more often and will have a greater meaning and impact on most of your one-on-one interpersonal communication. In the remaining two chapters we'll discuss the other categories. Few nonverbal books list more than 10 different signals even though most of these books are valuable contributions to the subject. Some nonverbal or body language books only list five different nonverbal signals.

Most nonverbal specialists write that in a first time meeting the 'tone of voice' will constitute up to 35 percent of the message you are communicating. It is also believed, by most nonverbal specialists, that as high as 60 percent of the remainder of your 'first time' message is given by your nonverbal signals 'without' one spoken word. The sum of these numbers is a provocative message nearly 'ninety percent' of a first time meeting is mainly communicated without any spoken words. I don't know how these statistics can be calculated, but certainly a majority of the message of a first time meeting is by everything except the words you speak. So it seems important to know as much about nonverbal signals as possible.

While working in this field, it is clear not everyone connects to the significance of this subject. Some people simply think it's fascinating and forget it. It is the author's opinion that those who have been exposed to the subject, of nonverbal communication, could be categorized as follows:

10% love the subject, understand it, and use it to make positive changes

80 % love it and use it in a modest way

10% didn't get at all

Be advised, your nonverbal signals are both helping and hindering your communication.

CHAPTER 13

SOME OF THE MAJOR NONVERBAL SIGNALS

Gestures – Expressions – Silence – Eye Contact
Mirroring/Leveling - Listening – Tone of Voice

GESTURES

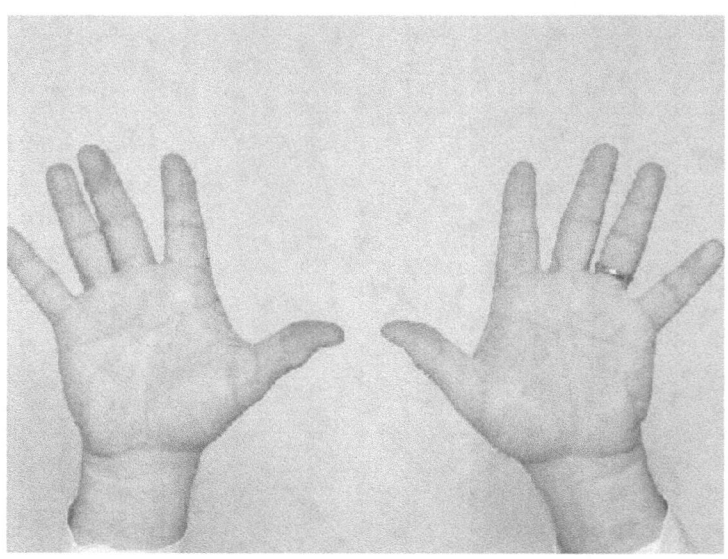

Few can count the gestures they make. Gestures mean the movements of hands, fingers and arms. The arms are almost exclusively on our body to place our hands and fingers where we want or need them to go and where we sometimes unconsciously place them. Our hands have no muscles, but have significant value for nonverbal communication and important tasks such as writing, eating, cleaning and communicating. One of the first important books on nonverbal communication is Body Language which claims 'hands and legs have a language'[1] I agree.[2]

This author writes about our hand movements both those we can control and those we do unconsciously. When male adults are under stress, they may chew on the tips of their fingers nails. Sometimes men rub their fingers together. Women in stressful situations will frequently place their hands over their mouths or chest.[3] Author Julius Fast suggests that these gestures have a truthful and exact meaning every time they are seen. Sorry Mr. Fast, you can't prove that. From many years of

1   Body Language, Julius Fast. Pocket Books division of Simon & Shuster, Inc. 630 Fifth Ave. NY, NY 10020, 1975, p. 145
2   Anthropologists at Columbia University in the early 40's studied man's gestural patterns. They found that they could discriminate differences among first-generational immigrants from Eastern Europe. (Book by David Efron, Gestsure and Environment (New York: King's Crown, 1941 republished as Gesture and Culture (The Hague: Mouton, 1972) The Italians were broad, full-arm gestures while Jewish immigrants tended to use movements close to the body, movements that seemed to trace the flow of what was being said. They also found that among the second generation, these unique gestures began to fade.
3   Ibid p. 145

viewing these important signals, this writer would unequivocally say, gestures may have exact meanings.[4]

Some gestures are for grooming ourselves. Some may bite their nails because they have a hang nail and want to remove it. We may bite our nails because we are nervous. Many people are constantly rubbing their arms, legs, stomachs or mouths.

Everyone has seen people who, when sitting, bounce their legs up and down unconsciously. It is my opinion this nervous bounce can also mean they have something important to do. Or they simply can't sit still. When I mentioned this signal to a very close friend of mine, he said, "I have done that since I was a little boy and it's always because I have to go to the bathroom."

What do you think the next five pictures communicate? All are common gestures. They are very subtle versions of the same gesture which you NEVER want to miss, especially when you're talking.

All five of these gestures 'may' be giving the same STOP TALKING message. These signals are much more respectful than their verbal counterparts!

---

4   Ibid p. 146

The five gestures pictured above all mean "STOP–I WANT TO SPEAK!"

Notice how these gestures can be seen very subtly or in more direct messages, gradually becoming the last and very clear message of stop.

Be advised that all of the subtle and quieter gestures in the first four pictures are just as meaningful as the big and very obvious message in the last picture.

To use the last gesture for stop is more difficult for most people because they don't want to be offensive.

The first one may not always be seen. We use the more obvious or clearer signals when the others don't work.

What gestures would you make for: I'm hungry – I don't understand – You're wrong – Go – Stop – Come – I don't agree – I'm thirsty – Goodbye – What? – I'm really upset about that – I like you – What time is it?

I hope you were able to see each one of these signals in your head. Perhaps you thought of some nonverbal gestures when you read some of the messages just mentioned?

Here are more gestures with clear messages:

Here is a familiar gesture, the placement of one finger(s) over one eye. Have you ever seen this gesture? When you do see this gesture, you probably think, "Their eye must itch." And many times you would be correct. But, when you see this gesture while you are speaking, it may mean they can't see what you're talking about. So when you see this gesture, stop talking and find out if they understand what you just said. Obviously, if they answer 'yes', then just continue talking , but you know they understood.

Here is the same gesture of several fingers over one eye. Many of us do one or the other of these signals to say nonvebally, "I don't 'see' what you are saying. We actually blind one eye…maybe both eyes…to communicate that we don't understand what a person is saying.

Placing the entire palm over the eye may be the same message. Remember their eye could itch. When I see this gesture, I always stop talking and ask, "Was that clear?" Or, "Did you understand that?"

This gesture is simply flipping both hands, palms up, over your head as if to say, "I surrender." "I give up." "I won't argue with you." It is interesting that the surrender signal is quite similar for war prisoners. When surrendering in a battle zone hands will go as high as possible.

Here is another signal which is very often a clue of acceptance. It is the gesture of stroking the chin. This signal can mean the person has decided to "buy", to 'accept', or has 'agreed'. I have seen it many times when it clearly meant acquiescence. I have trained several sales people to watch for it and when they see it, "ask for the order". This signal has been confirmed by many sales people I have trained. So I am reasonably confident that it works. However, you need to be aware that when you see this gesture, it could mean their chin itches.

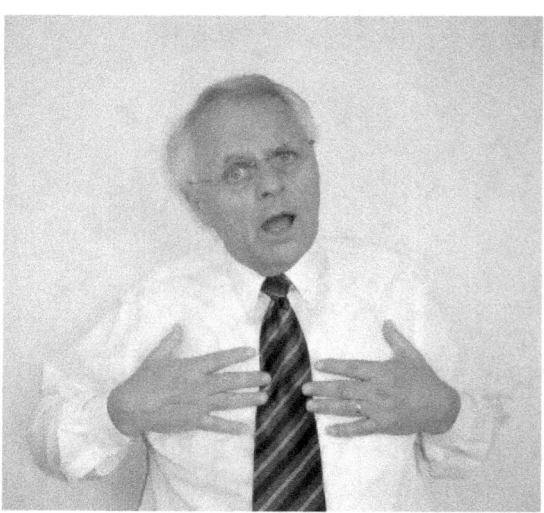

Here is a gesture which has many possible messages. The face usually confirms which message it is. One facial expression seems to say "who me?" Or the face could be suggesting, "You don't believe me?" Or, "You question what I am saying?"

Most people place their hand over their heart (truth speaks from the heart). Sometimes they will even pat their chest several times to convey an additional meaning of love and caring. It's a great gesture full of compassion, truth, forgiveness and acquiescence. It's a gesture of submissiveness, also.

Sometimes it is a great compliment of conciliation and agreement. For this nonverbalist, I like people who use this gesture. Almost always they are sweet people.

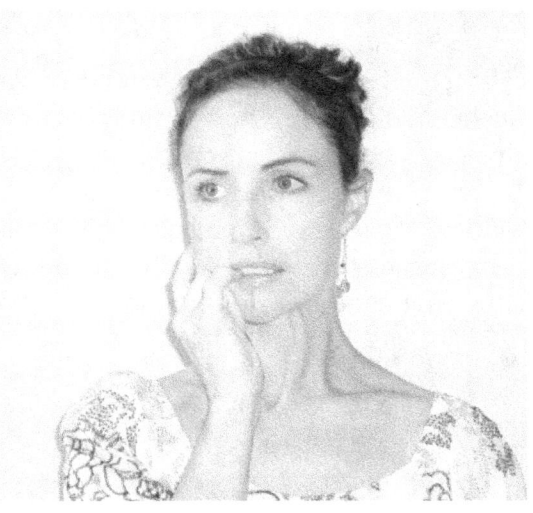

People will often place a finger or several fingers in their mouths when being pushed to do something they don't want to do. Sometimes they chew on their finger nails. Some body languages specialists believe it is a way to revert to the security of the child sucking on their mother's breast. Young children may suck their thumbs. When you see this signal, try to make them comfortable.

Just as a mother will hold a child close to their heart, often women will clutch objects such as a big chair pillow to find some comfort. Usually, when you see this gesture, they need some comfort; some reassurance that things are okay. I have seen men actually clutch a file folder and do it with a great deal of pressure, even bending the folder. This signal usually means nervousness or doubt. Again, for the record there may be a time when a woman does this for warmth.

Anytime you see a woman or a man literally open their coat or jacket and push it backward…then for men…place their thumbs into the belts on their sides as this photo shows, it means a fairly aggressive person.

Here is a consistent universal message in nearly every culture. The hands are raised with both palms up and back and both shoulders raised. Their head is usually tilted back and often their eyes are closed. Every time I have seen it, the message is loud and clear. They give up - they surrender. They don't want to argue.

Here is a sophisticated gesture in which the person seems to be rubbing his face or nose and blocking his mouth. This gesture usually is accompanied with the cluster of head down and looking away. With or without the cluster, the signals can mean the person is lying or telling a partial truth. They hide their mouth unconsciously. They scratch their face or nose because it probably itches. The itch is caused by a chemical called by the name catecholamines.[5] This fluid is secreted into the tissues of the nose and face which causes a slight itching. This chemical is caused from stress or anxiety. As I have and will say again, rubbing the nose may mean that they are lying.

But be careful, this is a signal which MAY have an important piece of information, but not always![6]

When both hands go over the mouth as shown here, it could mean they saw something terrible; they are afraid or they lied. Children rarely use gestures consciously or deliberately. They signal unconsciously and without any preconceived selection. Adults who are not used to lying and rarely do it may use this gesture when they are lying. Usually, this gesture in adults is fear.

5   The Smell & Taste Treatment and Research Foundation in Chicago. Dr. Alan Hirsch Founder & Director. Search Catecholamines On the internet go to smell and taste.org

6   Ibid

When you see this gesture, it probably means the person has made a decision or they don't need more information from the speaker. OR… they are simply now in a comfort zone. To know the difference you need to look at their face. Comfort has a pleasant, calm face. This gesture also can mean they are closing you out of their interest or reception. You might as well stop selling or pitching something you believe is important. Be careful here.

Another way to shut off someone is to discreetly cover their ears. I believe they do this unconsciously as it is too overt of a gesture to consciously do it. I know there are some big egos that do it because they don't care if they insult you. Sometimes they rub their ear rather than cover it. Both signals could mean you ought to change the subject or shut up. OH,…I almost forgot. It could mean their ear itches.

These American cultural gestures and their definitions are basically generalities with caution about exact meanings. However, they are gestures or body movement signals which can have exact meanings when seen. This writer has seen very few nonverbal signals with exact meanings.

Here are two very familiar nonverbal signals which are probably meaningful all over the world. The space flights helped spread these messages.

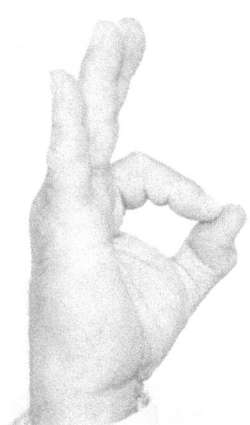

Can you begin to recognize that knowing about these signals and understanding their possible meanings gives you communication power? It is not a selfish or arrogant power, but a clearer and more meaningful communication power. You will communicate better, more precisely and hopefully more succinctly. You should be a significantly better listener and probably will use fewer words when you speak. For some people, they have discovered after taking my seminars that they don't need to talk as much as they used to.

Several recent seminar attendees have expressed that they feel more confident, say less, and are surprised that they NEVER saw these signals before.

SHAKING HANDS

The subject of shaking hands does relate to gestures, but because it can be a major nonverbal signal, I add this additional focus.

Until the late nineteen seventies women did not shake hands as frequently as they do now. This treatise will be focused solely on men. The most common statements about the subject are about men shaking hands with 'the wet fish handshake', the 'wimpy handshake'. Both of these comments are usually accompanied with distorted facial expressions; faces which telegraph feelings of 'awful', ugly', I hate it', 'yuk'.

These people should know that some people have occupations, which strong tightly squeezed hand shakes can harm or destroy violin and piano player's careers; surgeons and artists who can't risk injured hands and fingers. These people and others try to avoid shaking hands or do it with little to no squeezing. So...don't be too judgmental on these handshake gestures

The palm down handshake is covered in Chapter 21 and is one of the signals you can take to the bank when you see it. I offer this to those (especially politicians) who shake hands very often. Most Presidents shake hands thousands of times in one campaign.

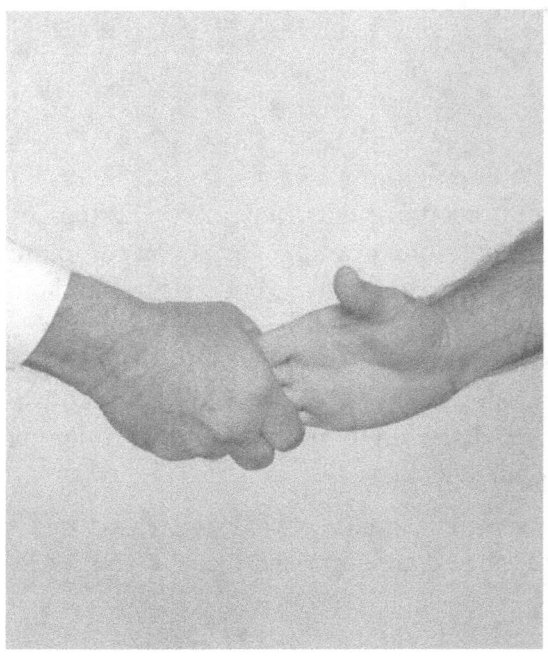

The President who SHOOK HANDS without ever having a sore hand was Harry S. Truman. The picture above shows how he quickly grabbed the other person's fingers thereby nullifying any power squeeze by the other person's grip. For those who are running for office, this is what you need to do to avoid sore hands, even injuries. John McCain's wife was badly injured after her hand was squeezed too hard and too often. She was in an arm sling for many days during her husband's 2008 campaign for President. If you are a violinist, physician or a concert piano player, you will avoid shaking hands every way you can.

There isn't enough space in this book to put every gesture I have seen. But the majority of those which you will see have been included. Keep your eyes open for some of these. Recognizing them will give you communication power! Again, knowledge of these signals can give you communication power.

REMINDER: these signals 'may mean', 'could mean', 'probably mean'. Sometimes they DO MEAN!

EXPRESSIONS

THE MOST COMMUNICATIVE
NONVERBAL SIGNAL

Expressions are part of the facial countenance. The eyes, eyebrows, mouth, head position and lips work together to form the myriad of nonverbal 'signals' - we call expressions combined. These signals can add light or darkness, calmness or anxiety to our countenance.

Our face is our message box, the loud speaker or whisper box; the static noise or song of our heart and mind. Our expression is mainly given by our face, but the eyes play a major part of expression.

The next series of photos (12 in all) depict various nonverbal signals. Using what you have learned, exercise your new found skills to identify them. Coming close is as good as getting it right. On a separate sheet of paper, match the feelings or messages with the 12 nonverbal signals shown from pictures A through L.

1. Aggressive 2. Fearful 3. Contempt 4. Sad 5. Disgust 6. Lost

7. Bored 8. Nervous 9. Authority 10. Surprised 11. Stalling

12. Disbelief (The answers will be at the end of this chapter).

A

B

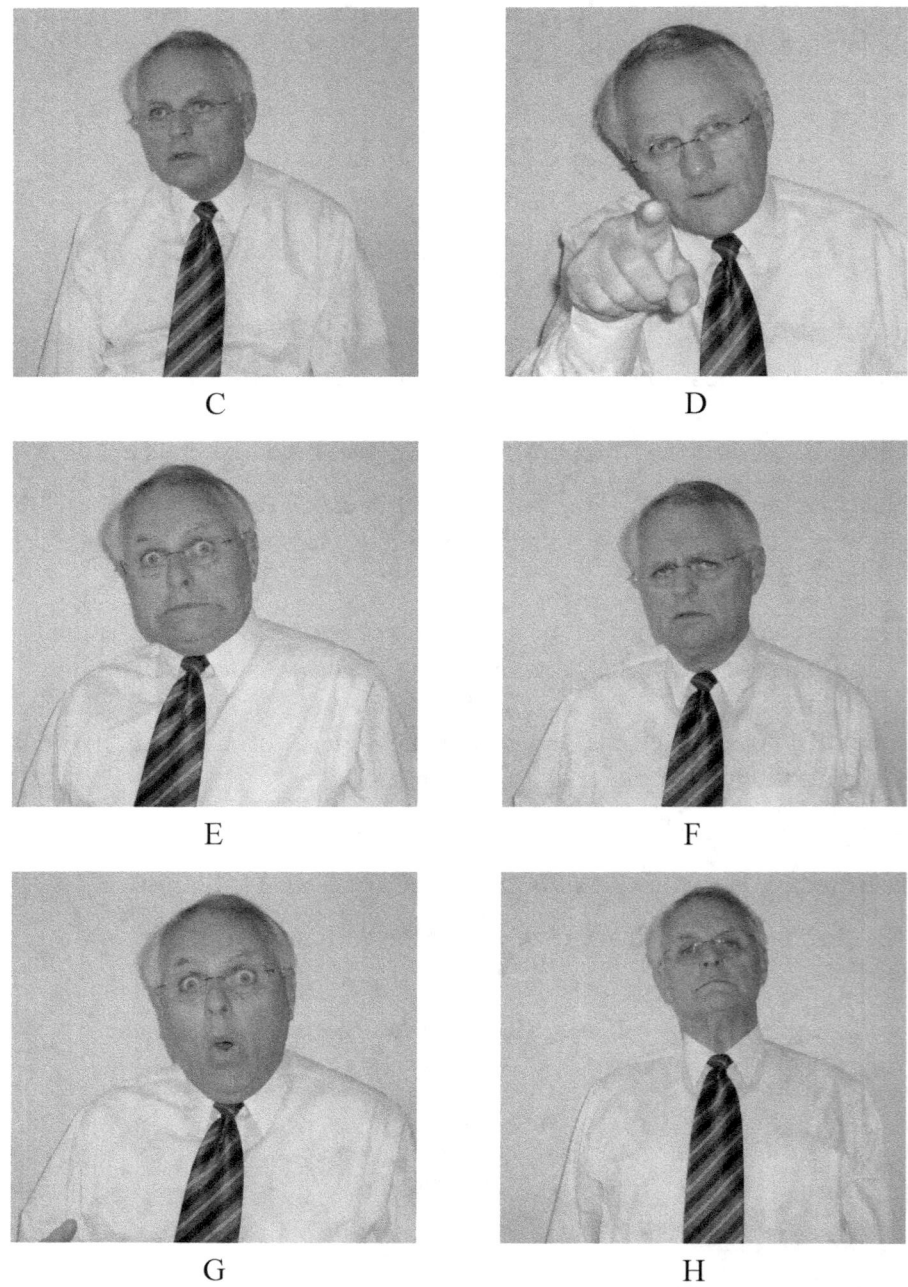

C

D

E

F

G

H

I

J

K

L

SILENCE

Silence says a lot. Obviously, silence is the absence of sound; when coupled with emotions it bespeaks the first sentence above. Let's take a quick look at an example of silence in action that happens maybe a million times a day.

Erik said something to his wife, Kym, and she was truly hurt by his words. Immediately, feelings arise and she is speechless. Not knowing what to say, Kym gives Erik the silence treatment; along with a cold stare. Erik senses the nonverbal communication is being employed here. Actually, he may not think those specific words, but he does know that his wife is sending him a message; a silent significant message that tells him that he's in the dog house. This particular story, which depicts an episode of silence used to communicate a feeling that was not verbalized, is but one way in which silence elicits a nonverbal signal.

Who is it during a conversation that must be most aware of silence? Interestingly, the person who does most of the talking is the person who should exercise awareness of silence. The settings that are being offered here involve sales people and job placement interviews. Essentially, the customer and the interviewee are in the position of doing a lot of listening.

For the seller and the interviewer, they are in a position of knowing and wish to let others know what they know. However, there comes a time, and it could be considered critical timing, when the seller and the interviewer need to be silent, not as a nonverbal signal, but out of consideration for the listener. The silence that occurs during a conversation between two people does not always have to be a signal that something is not going right, such as between Erik and Kym.

The most impressive leaders I have met were great listeners and had a greater amount of silence; even a silence which seemed programmed or consciously done. They simply spoke less.

There is an aphorism or maxim in sales which says, "First discover the prospect's pain, desire or needs. Then offer a solution to these pains or needs. Present all the benefits of your company's service or product. Tell them the costs. Then, ask for the order. THEN SHUT UP. The first person who speaks loses." This means if the sales person speaks first he loses the sale. If the prospect speaks first he usually decides to buy. This maxim is known as the magic moment in sales calls. It takes silence to make this maxim work successfully. I have seen this kind of silence last for minutes. I call it the 'closing silence factor'.

Interviewing new hires REQUIRES SILENCE.

Human Resource people often ask a question such as, "What do you like best about this field?" The applicant may, if allowed to talk long enough, reveal both good and bad reasons for hiring that person. By remaining silent it is very possible the HR person will gain information they need and information they didn't expect to get.

The following anecdote is an example. At a fortune 500 company on the outskirts of Washington D.C. I was reviewing the Human Resource

Director's interview with an upper level prospect for an important position.

One question to the applicant provoked an answer which included the phrase, "There's one problem you need to look out for in this business." Immediately after that statement, the Director interrupted the prospect which I thought was smart, since we needed to know what that 'problem' was.

But, the HR Director shocked me by saying, "May I interrupt you for a minute, I need to have my secretary change my schedule?" The applicant agreed and the HR Director left the room for a couple of minutes. Apparently this HR Director was head talking (head talking will be explained in chapter 17) about her own personal schedule and chose to break her silence. When we head talk during important conversations, we are vulnerable for remaining silent. We might as well talk out loud.

Although this head talking moment did not impact the decision to hire or not to hire someone, it could have been. I have seen many human resource people miss important information by NOT remaining silent in the interview.

Silence is in so much of our daily lives. Some of our nonverbal expressions communicate better with a pause of silence.

SILENCE IS ON THIS PAGE

Silence is to speech as the white space of this page is to the printed words printed here. Leaving space for a new paragraph has a message. The author is now going to change focus.

One writer says, physiologically, silence appears to be the mirror of the shape of discernible sound for each person.

The entire system of spoken language would fail without man's ability to both tolerate and create sequences of silence-sound-silence units.[7]

---

7   Journal of Communication Number 22, p 33 Harrison, R.P. and M.L. Knapp, 1972, Harrison also adds 'One of the great quotes on silence comes from a renowned author on the life of Christ. "As there was power in His actions, so was there power in His silence…" More about this subject in the book, Life of Christ, Frederic W. Farrar, published by Cassell & Company, Limited, London, England, 1874 p. 96

The power of verbalized words is dependent upon and requires pauses of silence. Some pauses we cover with noises which seem to keep others silent. These pauses are called filled or unfilled such as 'um', 'ah', or 'er'. We often use these 'sounds' to fill the space between our hesitations.

Then there are moments when we simply stop talking for effect. We often will silence ourselves to get a response or to get the person to think about what was just said. There is an interdependence of silence and speech for effective verbal messaging.

Harrison, in the Journal of Communication, writes that silence is in architecture, music, advertising design and parables of religious texts.[8] He believes Beethoven's 5th Symphony would not have the same power in the beginning without the three beats of silence. He believes some of Frank Lloyd Wright's architecture has silence in its design.[9]

Learn the power of silence and your production, success, happiness, communication will positively increase. Silence is the best balm for some friendships, business relationships and marriages, meaning we allow 'talkers' to talk on for long times, repeating themselves and giving us details we don't want or need. In other words, we stay silent to give others the opportunity to do what so many love the most, talking. That is friendly silence.

EYE CONTACT

Eye contact is a major part of our expression. Eye contact means when two people are looking at 'one of the eyes of the other' at the same time. You cannot look at both eyes of another person ever. So all of us pick one of the person's eyes and stare, glance back and forth or as in some occasions rarely look at either eye. These moments when two people's eyes are connected is called 'eye contact'. Some people have great difficulty giving or accepting eye contact.

Not making eye contact while listening or talking often signals self consciousness and/or insecurity. People who instantly like each other on a first meeting almost always have an excellent and locked-in eye contact.

8   Ibid Journal of Communication Number 22, p 34
9   Ibid Journal of Communication Number 22, p 35

When we meet someone we don't particularly want to spend much time with we usually avoid eye contact. So be careful not to communicate negative feelings with poor eye contact, even when you don't like the person. Be patient with people who have bad eye contact particularly in a business meeting. This probably will improve an unstated 'good feeling' from the one who gives little eye contact. Those people who are insecure feel more comfortable talking to people who give less eye contact.

Eye contact is expected by most of us. When we expect it and don't get, we are uncomfortable. It is common for some people who don't get good eye contact to shorten their time spent with that person.

Eye contact is a nonverbal acceptance signal from both parties. If you are afraid, or have difficulty looking others in their eye, then try changing that habit. It may be difficult, but it will be worth it. People connect so much better when there is eye-to-eye contact. One writer of body language said, "Without good eye contact, you might as well have both eyes closed."

MIRRORING OR LEVELING

Both terms are used because they have a slightly different meaning. Mirroring usually means copying gestures, stance, movement, sitting position, head movement and eye contact. Some body language writers use the term 'imitator' which, interestingly, is the original Greek word for our word 'mimic'. Aristotle gives a very interesting definition of imitation; another word for mirroring.[10]

Leveling mainly connects to the copying of the tempo of movement or gestures and especially to the loudness or softness of the voice. If you are talking to a person with a breathy voice, one without using much of the diaphragm, you can level to their tone by using a softer voice.

One who is louder gives you the opportunity to level by speaking louder. Mirroring and leveling are subtle compliments…BUT, don't get caught at it or it may be misunderstood; might even be rude.

It is true that when a person sees similar nonverbal messages from the person they are talking to, they may feel more comfortable. One major real estate company teaches mirroring, but fails to mention it could be

10   Aristotle Poetics, S.H. Butcher, Dover Publication, Inc., United Kingdom, 1951, p. 121

a problem if seen by the other person. Be careful with these nonverbal signals.

LISTENING

Listening is the greatest compliment you can give another person. From a life-time of counseling people about their nonverbal signals, listening probably is their biggest challenge; for some, their worse problem. A good listener is a great leader. A bad listener is talking and hearing mainly themselves…usually. The problems of listening are dramatically explained in Chapter 17 - Your Four Talkers.

TONE OF VOICE

Tone of Voice can have a major impact on a first time meeting. Many researchers claim that the tone of our voice represents as much as 35 to 38 percent of our impressions of a first time meeting.[11] Many people form strong opinions about a person based upon their voice.

The researcher G. L. Trager writes of paralinguistic or vocal phenomena such as pitch, range, vocal lip control, glottis control, pitch control, articulation, rhythm control and resonance tempo, all which play a part of our nonverbal signals.[12]

Some people talk too fast. Some people have a whining or a possible trembling voice; or a sort of vibration. Some have tense or breathy voices; some raspy or throaty voices. All of us have heard a nasal voice. We rarely forget the male orotund voice; clear, strong and deep. The orotund voice can also be bombastic or pompous.

Some voices are rough on our ears. There is little to nothing we can do about the tone of our voice, but we should know our voice does have a nonverbal value, which can impact a first time meeting.

Insecure people have fewer verbal messages and exhibit fewer expressions. However, they might be very expressive at home around people they know very well!

---

11   The Power of Body Language, Tonya Reiman, Pocket Books, New Yor, Toronto, A Div of Simon & Shuster, Inc. 1230 Avenues of the Americas, NY, NY, 10020, 2007, p 27

12   Nonverbal Communication: The State Of The Art, Harper, Wiens, Matarazzo, John Wiley & Sons, New York, 1978, McGraw-Hill Book Company, 1971, p. 21

ANSWERS TO NONVERBAL SIGNAL QUIZ

1. Aggressive is D   2. Fearful is E   3. Contempt is B

4. Sad is F   5. Disgust is I   6. Lost is C

7. Bored is K   8. Nervous is A   9. Authority is H

10. Surprised is G   11. Stalling is L   12. Disbelief is J

Many more facial expressions could have been included, BUT, to get the message you need to see the cluster of other signals, body movement, gestures or angle to correctly or nearly correctly get the intended message.

Some faces of people are very expressive, some are not. There are those who use many expressions while talking and when they are NOT talking…meaning they have many expressions while they are also listening; even on the telephone or in a face-to-face conversation. Those who are very expressive are almost always out-going and very verbal people; probably they talk too much!

"Well done!"

CHAPTER 14

THE EIGHT SIGNIFICANT NONVERBAL SIGNALS

PROXEMICS - POSTURE - TIME - PHYSICALITY MOVEMENT - ANGLE - DRESS - ARTIFACTS

The eight SIGNIFICANT nonverbal signals have value, but are not as important as the major eight just discussed. However, there will be times when one of the following signals may have as much importance as the eight major ones. It may depend upon there being a cluster or more than one signal at a time.

PROXEMICS

Proxemics is a term crafted by Edward T. Hall, explained in his book, `The Silent Language'.[1] Hall writes about the space around and between people and things.[2] Space can communicate messages of status. That which is more important is accorded more space. The important man has a big office, high up in the corporate building. The town's tycoon has a big house on top of a hill. The important printed message in advertising is presented with a lot of space around it and most likely this printed message is placed near the top of the page. Interpersonal distance, for example, has been seen as a cue of liking or disliking, trusting or distrusting, fearful or not, interested or not.[3] Hall lists four human distances:

intimate = zero to 2 feet, private = 2 feet to 3 feet, social = 3 feet to 5 feet, public = beyond 5 feet

---

1   The Silent Language, Edward T. Hall, Fawcett World Library, 64 West 44th Street, NY, NY, 10036, 1959, p. 13. Hall lists four human distances: intimate = zero to 2 feet, private = 2 feet to 3 feet, social = 3 feet to 5 feet, public = beyond 5 feet
2   Ibid p. 13
3   Ibid p. 24

All of us live in our own space bubble. We always carry our space bubble with us all the time regardless where we go. We use our space bubble at banks or ticket lines. Some people try to keep others out of our bubble. Imagine two strangers meeting for the first time. One has a big space bubble and is standing almost five feet away. The other person has a smaller space bubble and desires to be closer. The second person might even move closer only to notice the other person slightly backing up. The person who has the larger space bubble may now feel uncomfortable and may talk less or might even end the conversation to get this person out of their bubble. In business we need to use the 'social distance' described by Hall or we might negatively affect the deal, negotiation or interview. Our space bubble came from our culture and our traditions. Almost everyone who has a large space bubble is a non toucher. Touching and non-touching is explained in chapter 18. Hall's first book changed our Foreign Diplomatic Training.[4]

The husband and the wife had their own home spaces, which the other person quickly learns not to invade or touch or move. All of us take possession of certain space. We own it and don't expect anyone else to disturb this part of our space. Even animals have an area which they claim to be their own. In the book *Territory Imperative* the author claims that animals actually mark their territory. Lions might have thirty square miles.[5]

---

4   Edward T. Hall "Why Are We 'Ugly Americans?'" P 64. Hall wrote,"Though the United States has spent billions of dollars on foreign aid and programs it has captured neither the affection nor the esteem of the rest of the world. In many countries today Americans are cordially disliked; in others merely tolerated." The reasons for this Hall observed are many and varied, but he added that 'much of their foreigners' animosity has been generated by the way Americans behave." He mainly meant unconscious, rather than conscious behavior, and The Silent Language (his first published article) was a first attempt- many by Hall and his fellow workers followed- to analyze it. In the fore mentioned article published in Science Digest in 1962 Hall writes, there is a difference in time, space and friendship between Americans and other cultures. US citizens found it hard to adapt themselves to houses and offices arranged so differently, and often said there was too little or too much space, and often that too much space was wasted.

5   Territory Imperative by Robert Ardrey, Cambridge University Press, 1992 Territory imperative or equal ownership of the desk, table or restaurant setting creates many fascinating nonverbal signals. When a couple sits at a table in a restaurant, both unconsciously divide the table into two equal territories. Both will keep all their utensils, glasses and hands out of the other's territory. If you are with a friend and want to have some fun, simply and unnoticeably, assume more of their territory. Place your glass down slightly inside their territory. Every time I have done

Hall writes that Arabs, who thrive on close contact and are a touching culture (even holding hands while they talk), are very different to Americans and the British.[6]

POSTURE

Posture can make or break some professional job interviews. Improved posture can also improve one's self image. Posture is also the easiest signal to see in people, though it is striking how few people see bad posture. Those with good posture create positive words about a person and never mention the word posture. It seems both negative and posi-

---

this, they will pull their table mat toward themselves to own less of the table. They might even push their chair backwards also. It's fun with a friend, but rude with someone new. Remember the dividing rule and respect their territory and there will be no problems.

6   The Silent Language, Edward T. Hall, Fawcett World Library, 64 West 44th Street, NY, NY, 10036, 1959, p. 18

tive posture messages can't be recognized every time, even when their posture is an obvious message.

The way a man walks, stands and sits is often a message about them. We can see confidence, energy or even fatigue. A person can lean forward when talking to someone else or even lean backwards. All of these posture signals have their own messages.

In some cultures it is necessary to bow to others or sit at the feet of their elders. Some people cannot change their posture because of physical ailments or accidents. But poor posture, in many situations, can signal a message of indifference or arrogance. Another believes posture is a clue to character and an expression of attitude.[7] Another suggests that when two people are standing together it is not uncommon for one of them to mirror or copy the other's posture unconsciously.[8]

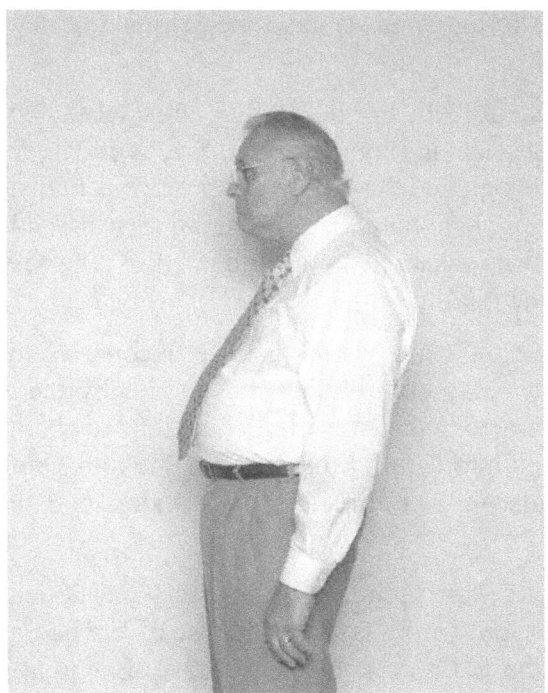

Posture is almost as identifiable as someone's voice. This writer can recognize people from a long distance by their posture. Flora Davis

7   Inside Intuition, Flora Davis, Signet Book, New American Library, NY, NY 1971, p. 93

8   Nonverbal Communication: The State of the Art, Harper, Wiens, Matarazzo, A. Wiley-Interscience Publication, John Wiley & Sons, New York, NY, 1978, p. 136

is one of my favorite authors on nonverbal communication and she writes, "A man's posture recalls his past."[9] embedded in our posture.[10] I agree. Another agreement I have with Davis is that a period of depression can damage a person's posture, but when that depression is removed, the bad posture remains…probably forever.[11]

Weak postures in our youth are not uncommon and for many, it stays with them for life. It is also true that as some people become successful they may exhibit better posture. Young girls, as they develop breasts frequently destroy their posture trying to hide themselves.

One example of this was at a university Theater Department where I taught. An attractive young girl with a great singing voice would slouch as she sang to hide her large breasts.

The stage director, without recognizing her problem, simply placed her in the back to hide her because she exhibited a negative message to the audience.

I knew this student well, so I decided to delicately talk with her about her weak appearance on stage and why. She admitted she tried to hide her body and recognized that this weak posture actually negatively affected her singing. Knowing that by leaning forward actually squeezed the diaphragm, she assumed an upright posture. The result was an improvement in the quality of her singing.

The transformation was enormous and unconsciously the director moved her down stage to give her more focus by the audience. Surprisingly, the director asked me what I had done to change her singing. I chose not to go into detail. I just told her she looks stronger on stage when she stands up. The director never understood the change was posture.

My own daughter wore large, baggy sweaters and slouched all the time and it made her look very insecure because of her bad posture. I mentioned it and she got a little upset with me. Eventually she decided good posture was a better choice and her self confidence increased with the better posture.

---

9   Inside Intuition, Flora Davis, Signet Book, New American Library, NY, NY 1971, p. 93
10   Ibid p. 93
11   Ibid p. 93

AN ANECDOTE ABOUT POSTURE
FROM MY ONE-ON-ONE COACHING

MATT: HIS WEAK POSTURE WAS
CHANGED BY A FAMOUS ACTRESS

For one month during a past summer, my nephew Matthew and I toured from Chicago to Boston to New York. Matt is an extremely handsome young man, very glib and outgoing. However, all those qualities suffered somewhat by his bent-over posture. I had asked Matt to walk with good posture and told him how it improved his looks. He did this for awhile but soon slipped back to his previous behavior. I asked Matt to give this new persona a name so when I saw him slouching I would say the new name.

He selected the name Zack. So every time he slouched, I would say, "Zack", and he would stand up straight.

Then my son came to the city accompanied by his very pretty date, a successful movie star and we all decided to go to dinner.

Matt was very impressed with this movie star from a major Hollywood Studio and asked many questions about the movies she had worked in. As we were walking on the un-crowded sidewalks in New York, I had an idea. I asked the very attractive movie stand-in to watch Matt as he walked and I told Matt to walk like his old self. After a few steps I asked Matt to walk like Zack. Matt became upright with excellent posture. He looked very handsome. I asked the movie actress whom did she like, Matt or Zack. The actress spontaneously and very effusively, raved about how wonderful Zack looked. Matt beamed and loved the attention he got.

Matt never walked like the old Matt again. That incident was about 10 years ago and Matt still stands tall and walks tall. When Matt got home, his parents almost didn't recognize him. It's a simple story with a great lesson. Good posture is a loud nonverbal signal and can work wonders sometimes. Walk tall!

TIME

Each of us has a natural rhythm of time. We eat, sleep and watch specific TV shows at certain times. We even rearrange important schedules to see a particular program. Our heart beats and our lungs take in air. In America appointments must be on time. In South America, you can be even hours late. Edward Hall writes in his book about two Arabs deciding to meet in Mecca and tour the Islamic sites, but neither mentions the day, month or year when they will do it. It could mean ten years later.[12] In Arabic countries a man never requires a specific time for others.

The subject of time is basically ignored by almost every author on the subject of body language. In my library are many books, but only three mention the silent messages of time. All of us use time, buy time, forget time, sell time and mainly waste time. Edward Hall writes in Silent Language, that there is a informal time, which means events will take days, months or years. Formal time is measured by calendars and clocks.[13]

As a former television director, I became extremely conscious of the length of thirty seconds. I can still close my eyes and open them after sixty seconds and rarely miss it by more than a couple of seconds. A telephone call at three in the afternoon is much less impacting on our minds than one at three in the morning.

Flying long distances disrupts our internal clocks. Our stomachs rumble when we are hungry. On long overseas flight we need time to ad-

12   The Silent Language, Edward T. Hall, Fawcett World Library, 64 West 44th Street, NY, NY, 10036, 1959, p. 103
13   Ibid, p. 105

just our body clocks. Time is a valuable part of our lives. We can kill time; take time, use time, waste time and measure time. There is formal time; we'll do it at eight o'clock sharp. A solar year (the longest) is 365 days, 5 hours, 48 minutes and 45.51 seconds. The sidereal year is shorter. Being late can cost you.

Sometimes thirty minutes late can change your life. Or make you rich. The American Patent Office received Elisha Grays design for the telephone on the same day as Alexander Graham Bell submitted his patent for the telephone, but Grays patent was thirty minutes later. It changed his life. So, no one ever heard of Elisha Gray, who became a footnote in history. Several lawyers got rich fighting over these 30 minutes. It made them richer.

Twelve seconds was the length of Wilbur and Orville Wright's first flight on December 17, 1903. Fifty years later, we flew into space. Sixty six years later we landed on the moon.

PHYSICALITY

The physical body shape, size and appearance are clearly important nonverbal signals. Some of our physicality we cannot change. Some people are tall and imposing; others are short and less imposing. We can't change our body structure. All of us know as we get older we usually lose our good posture and gain weight. If you can change your appearance by diet and exercise do it. Birdwhistell believes that we learn our looks – we're not born with them.[14] He sites the claim that often a husband and wife often learn to look alike and sometimes dog owners seem to look like their dogs. That is a stretch in most cases.

In the Nixon/Kennedy TV debates, it is believed Nixon lost the debate because his body looked wooden and tired while Kennedy looked vigorous, energetic and positive. Some believe that is why Kennedy won the election.[15] But don't let your physicality become an unnecessary

14   Introduction to Kinesics and context, Ray L. Birdwhistell, University of Louisville Press, Louisville, KY, 1952, p. 78
15   Kennedy was rested and well prepared. Nixon was exhausted (ending his campaigning the night before the debates) Nixon looked unshaven, tentative and seemed nervous. ON radio everyone thought Nixon won, but it was television where this election was settled. Nixon used a makeup to hide his natural dark beard and the sweat of the klieg lights made this makeup run. Nixon was ahead in the poles until this first debate. He never recovered.

focus. Many people do nonverbal things to hide themselves. Large busted women often slouch. Short people often get louder vocally and use bigger gestures to draw attention themselves, mainly to compensate for their shortness. So, if you can't change it, forget about it.

The size and shape of our body affects our message. A fiery political message delivered by an extremely overweight man may be uninteresting to some listeners. I remember a university professor who looked gaunt, even cadaverous, who was very difficult to watch even though his message was excellent. His physical body interrupted or blocked out his message.

People who HATE their bodies will do nonverbal things such as slouch, give little to no eye contact, or in a one-on-one meeting will stand farther away than most. Often, the volume of their voice will be lower. Most often their posture will be worse. Negative feelings about themselves can create a 'nonverbal cancer' effect and unconsciously negative feelings often impact our entire being.

If you dislike your posture make an effort to change it. If you're overweight make an effort to change it. BUT...how many really happy people do you know who look like you? Many. It is a mind set.

Most likely they have decided to accept their physical bodies and to be happy with themselves. Their nonverbal cancer-like connections often heal and they're happier.

In hundreds of one-on-one coaching sessions I have done, I find too many people who "dislike", even "hate" their bodies and will eventually admit, 'they hate themselves'. This distraction gets in the way of being a successful parent, employee and employer. Your negative body focus can and often does impact your appearance and communication messages.

AN ANECDOTE ABOUT PHYSICALITY FROM MY ONE-ON-ONE COACHING

STEVE: SHORT IS OKAY...BUT NOT FOR STEVE

Steve was very articulate, always kept his word and was industrious. He also was very short and conscious of it, therefore a lifetime burden for him.

His office was a 'loud' nonverbal symbol of his burden. Consciously he placed a three inch platform under his desk. Then he placed the side chair directly opposite his desk, but did two things with that chair. He cut the kegs off by two inches and had the chair screwed to the floor so no one could move it. When visitors commented on these chairs, he would dismiss it as something he had to do to keep his kids from removing them.

Steve probably didn't realize that this created a judge's bench setting for him. He had to be above everyone who came in. If he had more than one visitor, he brought out two other chairs also cut down by two inches. Sometimes when Steve had too many visitors, he would leave his 'exalted' desk chair and retrieve a special side chair just for him. This chair did not have the legs cut down.

I was invited to that office on two occasions. The first time I visited him, I deliberately stood in front of him as he sat in his chair behind his desk, which placed me above him. I quickly noticed he was uncomfortable and started to sit in the chair several feet away, Then Steve stood up. That seemed to remove the signals of discomfort.

Steve was well aware that I was a nonverbalist. On my second visit Steve took me outside to the back of his building and we sat at a table with an umbrella and regular chairs. As frequently happens, Steve asked me for some nonverbal observations. Problem! When I feel that the person asking for my observations will not handle them too well... or they are not teachable, I skirt the subject and basically mention very minor or insignificant signals. I was positive Steve was not really interested in my true thoughts. To his credit, he kept asking for more substance.

We finally went into his office where I pointed out the desk and chair messages. As unbelievable as it sounds, he was totally unaware that he had done that. I believe he knew what he had done. but tried and successfully put it in the back of his mind.

We talked about his father, who was shorter than Steve. Steve was aware that he wanted to be taller and above others...just like his father. His father had the porch swing raised over the other chairs by several inches. I met with Steve many times about his problem of 'being too short'. After I had decided I had totally failed in getting Steve to be okay with his shortness, Steve called me on a Sunday and asked me to meet him at his office. I said I could come on Monday and he wanted me to see his office with everyone else out of the building. So I went. His desk was now on the floor.

The side chairs which had been screwed to the floor were now closer to his desk without the screws. Steve decided he was okay being 'too short' (his words) and was going to try to forget it.

The easiest way Steve had of making changes about his hang-up was to make jokes about himself. One jest he would say is, "Steve, the shortest power in town". I had an opportunity of seeing Steve about 20 years later and I asked him how things were going. He said, "Great and I even threw away my platform shoes." Here was a man who had created nonverbal supports to overcome his fears and doubts. He now accepted his short-comings and moved on into an easier life, less complicated with silly but debilitating worries. He knows who he is and is just fine with himself. And it makes others more comfortable.

MOVEMENT

Movement is another nonverbal signal. Some people cannot stand still. They shuffle or move forwards and backwards unconsciously. Much of this movement is a distraction. Many people bounce their leg while sitting, but not many people see this movement. Others keep their feet constantly moving. Many people keep their fingers moving, rubbing, stroking and massaging their hands and arms, and some tug their blouse or shirt away from their body in repetitive movements. Simple movements…can have a profound effect on how we feel and think.[16]

Some people shuffle their feet or swing their arms when they want to get into a conversation. Their eagerness to speak is manifested by movement.

Nervous people almost always exhibit some kind of movement. Frequently, this kind of movement has no meaning at all.

Public speakers who exhibit excessive movement will most likely interrupt their own message. Perhaps you have seen a speaker who caught most of your attention with their excessive movement and you were unable to focus on the message. It proved to be distracting.

When your movement is excessive, EVERYBODY sees it. Most forgive it and ignore it. Some will not hear all of the spoken words because of this distraction. Often, when we are talking with someone who has a deadline or another place to be at that moment, they will unconsciously move backwards as they talk. When you see this 'backing up' movement, stand still and they might stop moving back, if they don't then say, "Well, I have to go so I will talk to you another time." They will be very grateful.

When your movement or another person's movement is obvious, then it becomes a nonverbal message, which may get in the way of good communication. People who are insecure will have less body movement, but they frequently have more erratic eye movement and movements of their hands and fingers. People who are outgoing and talkative will use more body movements while they are talking…and have many gestures.

---

16   The Outliers, Malcolm Gladwell, Litle, Brown and Company, Hatchette Book Group, 237 Park Avenue, New York NY 10017, 2008, p 63

Someone said, a moving tongue usually is accompanied with many moving body parts. That means talkers have more movements. Non talkers have fewer movements. When you are selling, keep your body movement at a minimum. You want the listener to stay focused on your message, NOT your meaningless movement.

ANGLE

Angle could easily be in the top list of the 8 major signals. However, very few people use the angle signal. Angle is turning the body away from a frontal position to a slightly sideways or to the most severe to a full sideways stance. Angle communicates several unspoken messages; "I want to leave." "I don't like you." " I'm more important that you are." Don't use angle EVER. Proud people, large ego types, and ignoramuses use angle.

The angle signal is usually given with other cluster signals such as looking away from the eyes of the other person or looking upwards and placing the arms and hands behind their backs. All of these signals are used to separate themselves from the one they are talking to. Almost every person I have seen give this signal has a very large ego and use verbal words of control and dominance. Hiding the frontal view seems safer for some. I have seen people use this angle position for awhile and then upon deciding that the person is 'okay', they turn back to the frontal position.

Angle is one of the signals which has a very loud and negative message. Angle can be used while sitting. It has the same probable messages. If I were a salesperson, I would NOT start my sales pitch with anyone at an angle to me. I would talk about the weather or whatever…until I have warmed them up a little…even until they face me front wise. Then I have a better chance of selling them…most likely. This signal is a powerful signal of arrogance.

Frequently, a person stands or sits at an angle deliberately, possibly trying to make someone uncomfortable. For some, it is a bad habit.

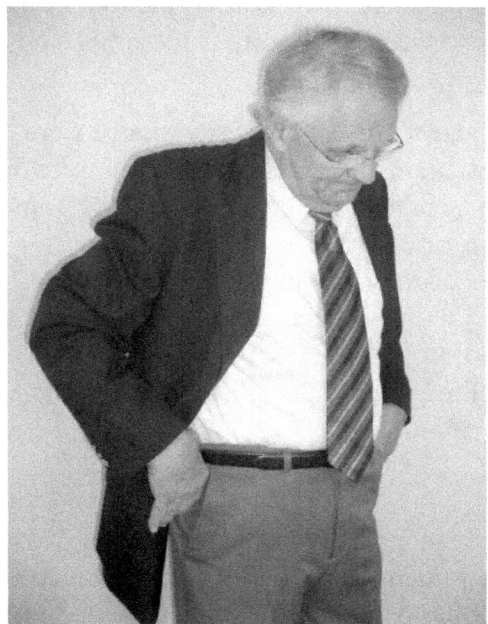

If you see this stance where the other person is at an angle, their thumbs are in the belt and their head is tilted down, you have trouble brewing. Don't be contentious and soften your voice. I know a body language consultant who says when you see this you should sit down some where. This gives the arrogant person the position over you he needs and it may soften the moment and eliminate, in time, the other person's arrogance.

DRESS

People arrange items in their home, office and vehicles, which present strong and clear nonverbal messages. Religious items may be hanging on the car's rear mirror. License plates and stickers silently give intended or unintended messages about a person's religion, sport's team or some cultural problem.

One's age may be a conflicting message to some because of the clothing they have chosen to wear. They may be too old to wear something suited for the younger person.

In adult communities, I have seen men wearing gold chains, bracelets, earrings and clothes that may seem to look better on younger people.

Many die their hair and wear wigs, all trying to look younger. Growing old gracefully is apparently abhorrent to some. These are nonverbal messages.

A few years ago, at a Midwest university, police were taken out of their uniforms. Their weapons were removed. They were dressed instead in blue blazers with a crest on the coat pocket. One immediate result was a morale problem on the police force. Many quit. The uniform was an important part of their self-image. Nearly every time there was a problem or a school disturbance, no one respected the authority being used. Policemen didn't have the same power in plain clothes. It wasn't long before the blue blazer was replaced by the police uniform again.

ARTIFACTS

Our flag is a major nonverbal artifact message. Most citizens do not want our flag desecrated. During WWI a mob forced a man of German extraction to kiss the American flag. He objected to kissing our flag. He said that the Old Glory was 'nothing but a piece of cotton with paint on it and that it might be covered with germs'. The case ended up in court in Butte, Montana and under flag desecration laws, the man was sentenced to 20 years at hard labor.[17]

Here is a famous artifact symbol. For 3,000 years, the swastika meant life and good luck, The word comes from the Sanskrit svastika, meaning 'good'. Even in the twentieth century, the swastika was still a symbol with positive connotations, but because of the Nazis, it changed

17   Nonverbal Communications, Randall P. Harrison Michigan State University Press, 1974, p. 78

the meaning to death and hate. Today, it conjures up terrible thoughts and feelings. Can there be two completely opposite meanings in one symbol? There are, but none are as paradoxical.[18]

AN ANECDOTE FROM MY ONE-ON-ONE COACHING ABOUT THE CLOTHES WE WEAR

Billy was a very handsome young sales rep with a major high tech company in San Jose, California. He was an immaculate dresser and very articulate. He was a great example of success. But he could not get many sales. When I was assigned to him as a coach, his boss said Billy has great days and then very bad weeks. When I met him I could see no problems at all and doubted that I could help him much.

We set a two day period when I would go along as a sales trainee. On the first day Billy made five different calls and did an excellent sales pitch, but didn't make a sale. I thought I knew the problem, but decided not to say anything until the next day. Billy was sick on that Friday so we postponed our next sales training session until Monday. On the third appointment, I was reasonably sure what Billy's problem was. Every prospect we visited was wearing very casual clothes and that is understated. It soon became clear that every prospect he visited was in work clothes or very casual. Was that Billy's problem?

I suggested Billy dress down, even a sport shirt. He agreed and I left town. About a month later Billy's boss called me and said Billy had only made one sale since the training I offered. He asked if I thought it was hopeless. I said let me call Billy and that I would get back to him.

I called Billy and he told me he just couldn't dress down...mainly because his wife thought he looked too informal. I reminded him that I had been helping sales trainees for thirty some years and was pretty confident he would do better dressing a little more like his prospects. He said that made sense, but...." I said, "Billy, do you believe your way isn't working?" He said it worked fine a few months ago. I told him he now had a different territory. He agreed to try it for one week. I

---

18   Ibid p. 78

hung up the phone with the thought, 'some people you just can't train or change'.

Two days later Billy called me and said he had closed five deals in less than two days....that he had seen seven prospects and took his wife out for lunch as well. He said he got all of the prospects he saw except two. Billy's prospects were all a first time sale. His home office did all of the follow up for further orders. He said his wife even told him to wear older shirts.

In a sense this advice fits the subject of leveling. When you seem too dressed up, too sharp and too 'perfect' for some prospects, your sales probably will be lower. How you dress does have value and in some cases, it makes all the difference.

CHAPTER 15

THE NONVERBAL MESSAGES OF THE OFFICE

A ROOM FULL OF IMPORTANT MESSAGES

Here are some of the important nonverbal messages which can be discovered in an office:

- Where the office is in the building
- The size of the office
- Where the office's occupant sits in their office
- The size of their desk
- What is on their walls
- Side chair and placement
- The best office I ever saw

As a nonverbal consultant, I have seen just about every office setting there is. Some are extremely difficult to conduct business in. Some are fortresses. Some are so small they diminish the perceived power of the occupant. Most offices I have been in are forgettable immediately after leaving them, which is probably good. Many offices seem to have personified messages. They seem to speak certain feelings or messages of hobbies, interests and travels about the occupants, even when he or she is not in the room.

I have met several times with a retired Admiral of the Navy in Washington D.C. who had many connections to the government, even as a consultant to the Pentagon. His secretary took me to his office and said the Admiral would be there in a moment. While waiting I had the opportunity of noticing all the famous people such as the current and previous Presidents and well-known military people he had his picture taken with. For me, these pictures gave me many messages such as

,'this man seems to be a family man', he seems to have a happy disposition', 'he's got a beautiful wife'. These photos helped me get a feeling of a man I had not met yet. The main one here was he seemed like an easy man to talk with. He rarely was the main focus of any picture, unlike many Senators' pictures I had seen. I learned a great deal about this military officer before he entered the room. All my impressions were confirmed shortly after he came in.

If you believe you are seeing a person of importance and one with the power to make important decisions, then that office most likely will be on the top floor and in the corner of the building and most likely it will be the longest walk to get to there. It will not be in the center of the building or on a lower floor! In government offices, except for four Star Generals and high ranking officials, most offices will look exactly the same. Some of the most powerful men in Washington D.C. have small and insignificant offices. So, excepting military offices, a great deal of information can be obtained prior to the actual meeting by looking around the office.

In the business world, the bigger the office, the more decision making power the occupant probably has. Unconsciously, executives actively seek, get or demand the biggest offices. Most people know that the one who gets the biggest office is usually the CEO or President.

Where the office is situated in the building can have an important message, meaning an office on a lower floor without a window rarely is where a decision maker sits. One time, on a sales training appointment with a new salesperson, we were told the person we were going to meet with was the decision maker. When we arrived, his office was on the first floor of a six story office building. Decision makers can have an office on a lower floors, but it is not common. This didn't fit with my experience, so quietly, I told the salesperson we might be talking to the wrong person. The new sales trainee was confident he had made the right appointment. The sales call took about double the normal time, because this potential client was also a 'talker', another signal this person was not the one to be meeting with. Finally, after about forty minutes the prospect said, "Well, you'll have to meet with 'so-and-so' before we can make a decision." Sales people need to know for sure who they need to see. These kinds of wasted calls can and usually do bring new sales people down and it doesn't take many rejections before they quit.[1]

The size of the office may have meaningful messages. Some offices are big because it is used for upper management meetings. Then there is a memorable story for me about the first shopping center to be built in Europe. It would be built in Neuchatel, Switzerland. I accompanied my friend Alexis, to a meeting with a major vendor in Geneva, who, we were told was very interested in renting space.

The man's office was large enough for a roller skating rink. While we were waiting for the occupant to enter, Alexis asked me what I saw in this extremely large office. Not only was the room big, but all the furniture was larger than most European offices I had been in. Even the pictures (original we thought) were large. I jokingly said, maybe the man we are going to meet is a big man and everything around him has to be big. We shared a laugh when suddenly in walked a man six feet five and at least three hundred pounds. He even yelled his name, Theo. His gestures were big and he stood very close to us when we shook hands. He was gregarious and very talkative. For me he was easy to read as everything he did was big and bold.

After about an hour, this big man excused himself to get a waitress to come to his office to take our luncheon orders. One issue we had left unsettled was which space his company would rent in the proposed shopping center. Alexis had previously said to me before we came to this potential vendor that he was saving the largest space for another

---

1   A few words about rejection in life. My father gave me some advice when I was in my teens. His advice can be summed up in thirteen words. For me it was great advice and worked extremely well. His advice was "It's not how many yeses you get, it's how many nos you get." In other words, when someone says no thank you, no, I'm not interested, forget it, or any other form of rejection, keep going, keep asking, keep trying to obtain your goal. Everything we have in electronics or which are very valuable to our modern society was thought of, discovered by, developed or created *after* many failures. The great maxim or truism about Thomas Edison's invention of the light bulb…is his chief engineer/supporter turned to Edison after their 1,000th failure and said, "Mr. Edison, we cannot invent an electric light." Edison is reported to have said, "No Sir, we have just identified a thousand ways which doesn't work. We need to keep trying." The story ends that it was on their 3,000th try that they succeeded in inventing the light bulb. Every successful inventor or successful human being got a lot of rejections before success! That advice from my father proved very profitable for me, and it will for you. It's *not* how many confirmations and yeses you get in life, but how many rejections, failures and 'nos' you get. Go get them!

vendor. I asked Alexis if the man he was saving the biggest space for knew that he was saving that larger space for him. He said they had talked about it, but no agreement was made yet and that company was much smaller than Theo's company. I told Alexis that if he offered the biggest space to Theo, he probably would say yes today. Alexis seemed reluctant. The discussion turned quickly to subject of what was the biggest space in the shopping center. Alexis looked at me and I signaled him to offer it. Alexis offered the man the largest space and the deal was done.

Alexis learned several weeks later that if this man had not gotten the biggest rental space he would have refused to be in the center.

It probably was true. A few days later, Alexis asked me if Theo's size had any connection to his renting the biggest space. It was a great question. I said, probably not, but I wouldn't rule it out. I told him it is not unlikely that a person's physicality is often reflected in items, furniture, cars, and business decisions. At any rate, it was a very unusual office and an interesting sales call.

Where the occupant sits in his/her office often has a nonverbal message worth noticing. If the desk is taking up most of the space and is centered in the room, we probably have an individual who consciously thinks about making a statement of power or control. Often, their own importance rating may not equal the company's rating.

Another time on a call with a sales trainee, we met a sales manager who had her desk and chair placed sideways to every visitor. This exposed her entire body and legs. I don't see that often. This arrangement is not common, but those who are comfortable about revealing their entire body in a business meeting are either very confident in who they are or spaced-out and disconnected to everything around them.

In this case, the woman was totally lacking an inflated ego. She was not 'into herself' and very comfortable with who she was. The trainee really liked her and so did I. She was a woman without guile, as they say, and every salesperson would be thrilled to have such a prospect.

Another training session I did was in New York City. I was taken on a sales call by the top sales person of a particular company. We agreed to say I was a sales trainee. Our call was a first-time visit to a new executive. So neither the sales person nor myself knew this person we were about to meet. It was an unusual experience. This salesperson had been told that the person we would meet was the main buyer for the company. As we walked into his office, which was fairly large, this man rose from his desk chair which was in the corner of the room, meaning his desk actually faced the corner. It was an unusual arrangement and jolted me somewhat. My first impression was this man cannot make any decisions. Luckily, before I could inform the man I was counseling, the executive apologized for his desk arrangement. He said that normally a large conference table usually was positioned in front of his chair so when he had executive meetings, all he had to do to be at the head of that conference table was to swivel around in his chair. This executive turned out to be a strong leader, very organized and our meeting was very brief and very successful.

The size of the desk can be an important nonverbal message. Some are so big they have to be brought in by cranes or special openings of the buildings. Some have to be dismantled and reassembled in the office.

What is on the walls can reveal a great deal of information. Senators in Washington D.C. are notorious for filling their walls with photographs of themselves with dignitaries.

One Senator from the Midwest has a reception room where there isn't enough space on the four walls for a postage stamp.

His picture with Presidents, military officers, foreign dignitaries and entertainers speak very loudly nonverbally. All these photos of him seem to say he needed attention and recognition. It is necessary to point out that he is not the only US Senator who aggrandizes himself with these kind of photos.

At one point in my career, I had to meet with many U.S. Senators and U.S. Representatives. I have only been in about fifty Senator's Offices, but most are filled with self images. The Midwest Senator's seems the best example. So what nonverbal message would this writer learn from his office? When in his office, talk about him and all will go well. Another Senator had enormous paintings on his walls, which became the first subject for most people who came there.

One Senator had a picture of a huge fish he had apparently caught. That was a great warming up discussion before I conducted my business. To their credit, all the politicians came from behind their desks to speak to me.

THREE ANECDOTES ON OFFICE SIGNALS FROM MY ONE-ON-ONE COACHING

MR. KEMMONS WILSON

The best office I have ever been in was the Memphis office of Mr. Kemmons Wilson, founder and former CEO of Holiday Inns. My appointment had been set. I was asked to take the elevator to his office floor and someone would be waiting for me. As the elevator door opened and before I stepped out a secretary said, "Welcome Mr. Grow, Mister Wilson is expecting you. Almost instantly Mr. Wilson stepped out of his office about twenty feet behind the secretary's desk and said, "Welcome Mr. Grow, please come in." I walked to his door as he stepped back and ushered me into his large, but unusual office.

I saw no desk anywhere. The only thing I saw were two soft, red couches facing each other right in front of me. Mr. Wilson told me to sit in the one on the left and he sat in the one on the right. We both sat in the middle of our couches. Between us was a small coffee table. When I left I noticed an oriental, bamboo screen where I assumed his desk was.

What this amazing man had done was to level the playing field or in this case, leveled the discussion area. Both couches had replaced the desk barrier and instantly made the atmosphere very welcoming. I had never seen that office arrangement before, nor since.

Mr. Wilson was the most polite, most endearing and most courteous CEO I have ever met on a business meeting. His autobiography, *Half Luck and Half Brains,* is worth reading. He gives great advice to his readers. He was a man in a million; a man without guile. He was and is the template for executives, managers and fathers. His nonverbal arrangement of his greeting area was an unexpected plus for a nonverbalist!

DR. JOHN
Doctor John was a psychiatrist
but nobody talked to him

John was a good friend in the 60's and 70's and when in his city, I would call him. On one occasion he asked me to lunch because he wanted to ask me something. At lunch he surprised me when he said his patients basically didn't talk to him. Impossible! Nobody was as friendly, easy-going and articulate as John. I didn't understand any of this.

As I was leaving, John asked me up to his office in a high-rise office building to see his antique desk. We went up. The instant I walked in, I knew why his patients were not talking to him. John's desk was huge. It was a fortress and it took up most of the space in his office. It was an extraordinarily beautiful antique desk, but it belonged in a museum, not in his office. He sat behind this fortress and his patients sat in a smaller chair slightly hidden on the other side.

I told John that as long a his patients had to sit behind his fortress, like school children being reprimanded or lectured to, they weren't going to do much talking. John knew instantly I was right. He then told me how expensive and how difficult it had been to get this fortress up and into his office. It had to be dismantled and brought up in a larger freight elevator. I advised John to place two chairs in the corner with a small table between them and his patients would talk to him. He did and they did.

An office can have friendly nonverbal messages or unfriendly non-verbal messages. It really matters what's in your office and what is on your walls. Think about your customers or patients before you buy your office furnishings. Some things shut people down. Some items make it easier to talk.

DERRICK
The boss has to look like the boss
even in his office

My friend Carlos had an appointment in Dresden, Germany regarding the first proposed shopping center in Western Europe. He asked me to accompany him. Carlos was told that Derrick was the man of power and influence for signing a major watch distributing contract for the new shopping center.

Carlos made several phone calls through Derrick's secretary to set up the meeting. After many telephone calls the meeting was set for nine in the morning the following week. On the morning of the meeting we went to a four story building which had the company's name on the facing of it. We waited in a lobby to be called upstairs.

We were advised by Derrick's secretary to come up to room 303 on the third floor; FIRST important signal. The power, meaning the person who can make decisions, rarely sits on the third floor of a four story building. Maybe, I thought, the upper floor was for another company. I noticed this signal, yet I ignored it. In foreign lands not all nonverbal signals speak with the same meanings as they do in America.

In a few moments we were ushered into Derrick's office (SECOND important signal) and were told Derrick would be there in a couple of minutes.

We were offered coffee, tea, beer or wine. No water, which I wanted. The second we were ushered into the office, I knew we were not in the office of a decision maker. The only desk in this small office was facing the corner. This meant that Derrick sat at his desk facing the corner with his back to the entrance. Two chairs were placed a few feet away on the opposite side of this small room. Instantly, I told Carlos we not talking to a decision maker. He tried to convince me that he had done the research and Derrick was the one we needed to sell.

I wasn't buying it. Derrick was NOT THE POWER and could not make any decisions. The nonverbal messages of that office confirmed I was correct. So when Derrick showed up, Carlos asked Derrick to convince him that his watches would sell in his stores, then he could make the deal.

Derrick graciously admitted he was not the decision maker and told us who was. We asked if we could see that person since we had traveled from Zurich the day before. Unfortunately, that man was out of town and wouldn't be back until the next week.

Carlos and I flew back to Zurich. A new meeting proved successful for Carlos and he signed an agreement to have his watches marketed at Europe's first shopping center.

Clearly, in America and probably most European businesses, the person of power always has the office position, setting and trimmings of importance. Generally speaking, if you want to locate the CEO of almost any corporation, go to the top floor and look for the corner office.

CHAPTER 16

FIRST 30 SECONDS TO 5 MINUTES OF FIRST-TIME MEETING

WHERE YOUR SIGNALS MATTER MOST

Some of the nonverbal and body language authors write about the importance of the first thirty seconds to five minutes of a first time meeting. It is a very critical time when nonverbal signals have the most important meanings. In the second meeting of two people, signals such as eye contact and body and head positions will have less of an impact. By the third meeting, these specific nonverbal signals probably have no impact at all and will be of little value.

FIRST MEETING EXTREMELY IMPORTANT WHERE WE ACCEPT, REJECT OR IGNORE NONVERBAL SIGNALS

For meaningful relationships in parenting, marriages, selling, negotiating and business, all of these first time signals that emerge between the same two people are when we reject, accept or patiently excuse them.

It is very possible that when we end a relationship because of a certain signal or cluster of signals, we may have lost a great friend or business relationship forever!

EXAMPLE: One woman I coached told me when she meets someone chewing gum; she rarely spends much time with them. She said, "I can't stand people who chew gum in a business meeting. Most of the time I don't spend much time with them." She agreed that she may have rejected someone who might have been a good customer. I reminded her that some people chew gum to help them stop smoking. She said, "They need to do that privately and not on my business calls."

These first few minutes can make or break a sale; notwithstanding, many sales people can overcome bad starts. It is often in these first few moments when the prospect decides if the salesperson is reliable, well informed, experienced or otherwise and if they will buy or not.

TWO ANECDOTES ON SIGNALS ABOUT THE OFFICE FROM MY ONE-ON-ONE COACHING

80/20 RULE AND NONVERBAL SIGNALS WERE THE PROBLEMS

Dean was the leader in making first time calls and he had one of the smoothest presentations among forty sales people. His boss asked if I would work with him because his production was never as good as less experienced, less communicative sales people in his organization. Dean was about forty five years old, very bright and very knowledgeable with a great countenance.

I couldn't believe Dean wasn't the top salesperson. Dean was very proud of his reputation of making the most calls on new prospects. That I liked...or thought I did.

Dean and I got into his car and I asked him how many first time prospects he had called on this month. He answered this was his sixteenth first time prospect call that we were going on. Although unknown to me on the evening before we went together on this sales call. He spent several hours studying about his company's new annuity product. Not a bad thing to do, but this particular studying of annuities was useless for Dean.

"What two strangers, meeting for the first time DO in the first 4 minutes is so critical, it will determine if they will remain strangers or will become friends or man and wife."

Shortly after meeting this first-time prospect, Dean asked the prospect if he could tell him about the company's newest product, annuities. The prospect said he was very aware of their new annuities and seemed impressed that the salesperson mentioned it. Dean was very happy and started to give details about that product when the prospect gave Dean a very important nonverbal signal.

In selling, there is the rule of 80-20, meaning, you get 80% of your business from 20% of your customers. Dean obviously knew nothing about this rule.[1] I recommend a great book on the 80/20 rule. The book is called *You Can't Teach a Kid How To Ride A Bike in a Seminar*.

The prospect raised both hands, palms out which is the signal to stop, but Dean either ignored it or, as I found later didn't see it. Dean continued pitching, rattling off more about the product that the prospect was clearly NOT interested in, at least not at that moment. The prospect subtly repeated this hand signal gesture again unseen by Dean. It wasn't very long before the prospect stopped looking at Dean and began talking to me. After a few pleasantries, the prospect announced that he was busy with something else and asked Dean to call him in a week or two. The sales call was over in less than twenty minutes. When alone, the prospect asked me if we sold a certain annuity. I said yes.

The prospect said he was interested in buying a certain annuity and to have Dean call him in a couple of weeks. I was later told that Dean did call this prospect a few weeks later. The prospect told Dean he had met with another insurance person and bought some annuities from him.

1   You Can't Teach A Kid To Ride A Bike At A Seminar, Bay Head Publishing Inc. 1999. p 63

What caused Dean to lose the sale? There were two reasons. First, Dean missed the 'loud' nonverbal signal to stop talking and listen. Secondly, Dean was focused on himself. Dean did NOT know what his prospect's pain was. What does this prospect need or want. Dean's sale call was as ineffective as trying to sell a refrigerator to an Eskimo, excusing the superfluous.

Dean had prepared himself the night before for a pitch and was consumed with what he wanted and NOT what the prospect wanted. I suggested that Dean read Emerson's essay on 'Law of Compensation' which focuses on service rather on selling.[2] Looking for other's needs requires asking questions and looking at nonverbal signals. When you go on a sales call to determine what the prospect wants, it's better to ask questions than to pitch a product you want to sell.

Dean called me about six months later and said he was listening and watching more and his production was up. He wanted information to help identify additional nonverbal signals of which he should be aware of. As often happens, Dean was now consumed by seeing every signal and I knew this could be a major distraction to his task of selling.

WHEN THE FEET HIT THE FLOOR MAKE YOUR PITCH

I was with a new salesperson whose boss told me he made five or six calls a day. But, his closing rates were low. So, I went on a call with this 'slick' salesperson. On the first call I saw his problem. So on the next appointment I told the trainee NOT to begin his sales pitch UNTIL I gave him a signal and until then he was to talk about the weather, pictures hanging on the prospect's wall or anything else. He was NOT to begin the sales pitch UNTIL I signaled him. My signal was me tugging on my ear lobe.

The sales call we first went on was a classic example. On the second call, we made introductions and then the salesperson started talking about everything except his product and was running out of subjects to talk about. He kept looking at me for a signal to begin his sales pitch.

---

2   Ralph Waldo Emerson: Essays and Journals, International Collection Library, American Headquarters Garden City, New York, 1968 by Nelson Doubleday, Inc. 112

I have reproduced in the pictures shown how the prospect looked and the slow and agonizing changes he made with his feet.

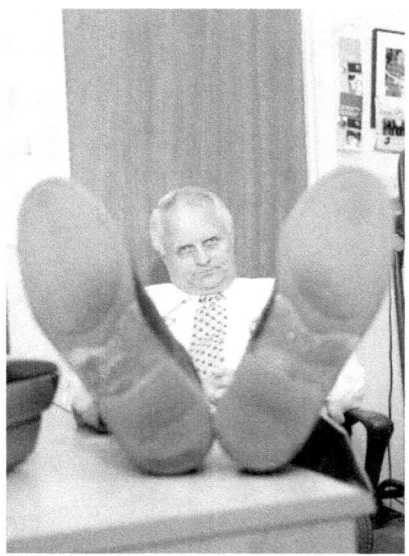

The prospect was sitting directly opposite from the salesperson with his feet up on the desk, basically talking between his feet while blocking the salesman's view of the prospect's face. It was rude to say the least, but true. The prospect kept his feet on the desk for a long time. The salesperson was running out of things to talk about.

In a few minutes, the prospect pulled out the top drawer of his desk and moved his feet down from the top of his desk to the first drawer. The salesperson was still looking at me hoping I would signal him so he could start his sales pitch. The salesperson managed to get the prospect to talk about his fun for flying, but his feet remained on the top drawer.

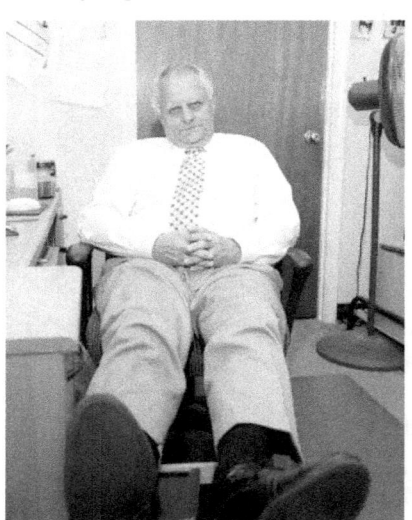

Sometime later, the prospect pushed in the top drawer and pulled out the next drawer and placed his feet on that drawer; still talking to the salesperson between his two shoes.

The sales person glanced at me, looking for the signal to start his sales pitch. Not yet! The prospect's feet were almost a nonverbal stop sign saying he wasn't interested in talking to this salesperson. He might as well have raised the crossing guard's top sign and held it up all the time.

Finally, the prospect pushed this drawer in and placed his feet on the floor. I gave the signal to the sales trainee and within thirty minutes a sale was consummated. We had been in the office for about an hour. Half of it was waiting for both feet to get on the floor. In fact, the prospect, who was very distant, arrogant and uninterested when we first walked in, turned out to be a very nice person and very talkative. After he made the purchase, he kept talking and we had some difficulty in getting out of his office. The prospect took time to show us all his airplanes. There are a number of stop signs sales people can get. This one was memorable.

There is a time when a salesperson should begin the sales pitch and there are times when it will be harmful to begin the pitch before a warm relationship has been established. The first 30 seconds to five minutes hopefully will get the prospect centered on the sales call so the salesperson can start his pitch.

The best advice I can give is if it 'feels right' proceed. If it doesn't, then do what you can to reach that 'feel right' moment. It takes two to make a sale. It takes two to succeed at a negotiation. It takes two to decide on a marriage. Don't waste your sales pitch on a closed-up prospect. You won't make many sales that way.

CHAPTER 17

YOUR FOUR TALKERS
AND THEIR RISKS

MOUTH TALKING
HEAD TALKING
NONVERBAL TALKING
TALKING OUT LOUD TO ONESELF

#1 MOUNTH TALKING

Mouth talking is the BIG problem for some people. Many job interviews are lost because the applicants have talked too much. Human Resource people often nod, lift their eyebrows or open their mouths to speak as a signal they are listening and in fact haven't heard a word... deliberately. They don't want to listen any more and rarely say "Please be quiet and leave". We should learn when to answer ONLY the question we were asked and do it with as few words as possible, which is responsive to the question asked and no more.

Many people feel that if there is a pause or silence during an interview, someone needs to talk and since they are in a job interview, it is nearly always the applicant who speaks first and often it is something totally unimportant or not connected to the question. In job interviews answer each question succinctly and remain silent. You DON'T have to fill the silence.

#2 HEAD TALKING

Head-talking or the power of thought, can be never-ending and extremely exhausting. Below is a list of many of those things which start these silent monologues. Some people must use drugs or mind altering stimuli to 'avoid' the sometime stresses of thinking or head-talking. While reading this paragraph, you are head talking this second. You can't stop it. So learn how to manage it. One way to overcome this problem is to concentrate strongly on what the other person is saying. And when you get a thought to interrupt…DON'T. This will help you become a better listener.

Imagine Bill is talking to Sue. Bill says something which really angers Sue, but she can't get into the conversation because Bill hasn't taken a long enough breath. So Sue starts head talking, working up her responses for Bill as soon as he does take a breath. What happens when Sue is head talking? She probably has not heard a word Bill has said since she heard the angry sentence or phrase which started her head-talking.

Bill takes a longer breath from his mouth, Sue jumps in with her well rehearsed head-designed response. But, her comment is totally unrelated and off the subject because it is now long past that original subject. As a result, Bill doesn't understand what Sue is now talking about. Head talking has blocked out her listening.

Head talking can be a problem for most of us. Kids seem less affected by it. They speak every head thought they have and every time they think of something new to say.

HEAD TALKING IN SALES

The problem with head-talking in a face-to-face, first time sales meeting is obvious. It can block out EVERY word spoken and even EVERY nonverbal signal given. You can't sell someone unless you "have heard" all the needs, requirements or the pain the prospect wants fixed. Head talking may be a sales person's biggest stumbling block.

What Causes Head Talking?

- specific buzz words - something which smells
- a sound you cannot identify - the clothes the other person is wearing
- the color of their eyes - their good/bad or lack of expressions
- their senseless movement - their teeth, hair, mustache
- their tone of voice - the volume of their voice
- their 'ahs' and 'dahs' - their 'you knows' repeated over and over
- the temperature or time - the next thing you have to do
- their bad grammar - the speed of their talking
- an unexpected interruption - you conclude they aren't listening to you
- they seem rushed - something smells
- they are talking too much - they seem to be gossiping
- a previous attitude about them - they usually waste my time

- they already said that - why don't they take a breath, so I can talk

- I rarely believe what they say - they mispronounced a word

In summary, what starts head talking? It seems just about everything and nothing at all. Professor Randall Harrison of Michigan State wrote, "Some of us see everything and some of us don't. Some of us hear every misstated word, bad grammar, verbal blunder, inappropriate metaphors and massacred idioms. Some brains can silently repair these distractions, but it is done at the expense of effective listening. How can anyone's spoken words pierce an eardrum when the brain is so busily engaged in judgment calls?"[1]

My grandmother had an expression which she said repeatedly encouraging others to consider: "Don't get diverted by what people say. Figure out what they meant. You'll have more friends." It's great advice.

HEAD TALKING ANECDOTE FROM MY ONE-ON-ONE COACHING

SUSIE: *ALWAYS TALKED WITH HER HEAD DOWN*

Like many who attend my seminars, Susie signed up to talk to me. Susie was very pretty, very glib and easy to be around. She had excellent communication skills, but inside she admitted she was uncomfortable around many men. She didn't like aggressive behavior, a 'know-it-all' or a 'loud mouth'. Who does?

Susie regularly saw a psychiatrist for depression and anxiety problems. She wanted to talk to me because she felt I was a good listener - a nonverbal conclusion before we ever met. She came into my room with great energy and style. She shook my hand firmly and sat down quickly.

I asked her some questions. The whole time she was answering these questions, she kept her head slightly down and at an angle. This negative nonverbal signal conflicted with the positive verbal messages she was giving. It was a mixed message for me. I stopped listening to her

---

1   Beyond Words: An Introduction to Nonverbal Communication, Randall P. Harrison, Prentice Hall, Inc. Englewood Cliffs, New Jersey, 1974, p.80

and was fixed upon her head position. I wondered how long she would keep her head down and at an angle. She never changed it.

I asked her to leave the room and come in again as I wanted to see her enter again. She felt uncomfortable until I made some kind of joke about it. She laughed and left the room. She entered it the same way, still with her head down and at an angle. I wondered why. Nothing she said or did matched her verbal messages. Her nonverbal movements were in constant disagreement with her verbal messages. I could not confirm anything and was totally at a lost why she kept her head down.

So I asked her, "Susie, are you aware that you have had your head down and at an angle the entire time you have been in this room?" She said, "I have?" never lifting her head. I asked if she was aware of that. She answered she wasn't.

I then told her I was going to mirror her as we continued to talk. So I copied her head position, down and at an angle and I did it for several minutes. Then I stopped and asked, "How did you feel about that?"

"I hated it."

"Why did you hate it?"

"I don't know …it looks odd or something…I just hated it."

"You have kept your head down the whole time you have been in here."

"I have?"

"Yes. Do you know why you do it?"

"No…I didn't even know I did it…that's weird…why do I do it?"

"I have no idea."

"Wow…that's crazy…I should stop it shouldn't I?"

"Why do you think you should stop it?"

"I don't want to look like that."

I asked Susie to hold her head upright as we continued to talk. She did and found it a little strange as if she had her head up too high. We agreed that when I had my head down and at an angle it looked odd to her. We agreed it was going to be difficult for her to remember to hold her head up.

I noticed that she wore small earrings and suggested that she buy a new pair of earrings which were too tight or a bracelet that fitted too tight and, on important meetings, that she wear this tight jewelry to remind her to keep her head up. She agreed.

The fascinating conclusion to Susie's unique incognizance is a letter she sent me saying (with her new head position) she met with her psychiatrist a few days after our meeting. The doctor was perplexed; he saw a different Susie. He did not notice that she was now holding her head up more. He asked her, "What have you done? You're different. You seem happier…more content. What have you done?"

For this writer, the doctor noticed a more positive nonverbal look with a brighter countenance. Both of these signals have a different and a more reassuring look. Susie finally told the psychiatrist about our session.

A head held high has a stronger positive message and since Susie wanted to make a change, she took steps to do so. In her case it had immediate results. I always wonder when I help someone make a major physical transformation, especially with minimal effort, if it became permanent. Later on Susie told a colleague of mine, "Meeting with Mr. Grow was the best money I ever spent." So maybe her change held 'up'.

#3 Nonverbal Talking

Remember that your movements, expressions, gestures and other nonverbal signals are almost always giving some kind of message to others. It is what this book is all about.

#4 Talking Out-Loud To Ourselves

Most people have moments of talking out loud to themselves. Some, after they have finished a face-to-face conversation start talking out loud to themselves privately to say the things we wanted to say earlier. It might be viewed as a means to rehearse for the next meeting.

Often, it is some issue that is very important to us, which stimulates these out-loud monologues. These unheard monologues can be important for future debates, conversations and interviews. Most of the time, we actually see the face in our minds-eye of those who we are talking to. This nonverbal phenomenon of actually seeing the faces of those we are talking to helps us develop our responses.

We can actually hear in our heads their responses. We can also notice their body language signals, all in our head.

After a seminar on this subject, I asked a question to those students who admitted that they talked out-loud to themselves. I asked if anyone actually saw the face of the ones they were having head-talk conversations with.

Here are some of their answers. "I saw her red dress which I hated". "I saw her crying at my words, so I changed my (out-loud) message." "I knew I was wrong and apologized to him...my boyfriend...first in my head and then later to him when I saw him, I apologized for words he had never heard."

Since my professor in college made me aware of this subject, I have been more aware of those who do it. One friend of mine, a first rank scholar and professor emeritus of ancient literature, said he talked out loud to himself all the time. He said. "There isn't an hour when I haven't had a conversation or an argument with myself or others out loud to myself and I do it everywhere...even in Church sometimes. I have even had arguments with some people who are a hundred miles from me. I usually lose the self-inflicted arguments I have."

PEOPLE WITH POOR SELF IMAGE DON'T OFTEN TALK OUT LOUD TO THEMSELVES

It is surprising that not everyone talks out loud to themselves. It appears from this author's observations that insecure people talk-out-loud to themselves much less, if at all.

Professor Randall Harrison of Michigan State was convinced that insecure people rarely did it. He believed that the best profile for those who talked out loud to themselves were those in academia, those people who were absorbed in writing, thinking and teaching. He knew so many professors who did it.[2]

---

2   Nonverbal Communications, Randall P. Harrison Michigan State University Press, 1974, p. 103

What is clear is that talking out-loud to oneself is rarely interrupted by anything or anyone unless another person invades their space. When 'out-loud talkers' see someone looking at them, they usually stop.

THERE IS A BENEFIT TO TALKING TO ONESELF

Harrison believed it was very healthy and productive in preparing a speech or a verbal argument in a debate since we seem to hear their comments in advance. This will help us develop a verbal strategy (in our head) when we get in front of another person. So, in a sense, we have rehearsed our future verbalization.

It seems that those who talk out loud to themselves about impending interviews or meetings are immensely more prepared. It is clear we practice for a marathon race by running long distances and measuring and monitoring our progress. Why wouldn't it be profitable to rehearse out loud a future important conversation? I talk to myself about certain chapters of a book BEFORE I write them.

Harrison said, "When you talk out loud to yourself you focus yourself intently on the challenge, situation, or circumstances." Put that in your head and talk about it.

CHAPTER 18

TOUCHING: ALSO CREATED BY TRADITIONS

EXTREMELY IMPORTANT NONVERBAL SIGNALS WITH THE MOST INFORMATION (AND RISKS)

By far the most profound nonverbal signal is touching. This subject I rarely talk about in my speeches and seminars. The only place I give this sensitive subject any time or focus is in my one-on-on coaching with those who have requested my counsel. Why? It is an extremely personal subject and often is difficult for my non-touching clients. Touchers can handle the discussion and information about this behavior much more easily than non- touchers. Non-touchers always have many more hang-ups about themselves, including being too close to touchers.

Why are some people non-touchers? Four reasons:

1. Non-touchers are raised by one or two non-touchers.

2. Non-touchers were placed in an incubator at birth or not touched by their mother or father or surrogate parents very often.

3. Non-touchers were abandoned at birth or placed in a foster home and rarely held.

4. For medical reasons newborns are in a hospital too long without constant tactile experiences. This unfortunate situation can change a person for life.

It seems obvious then why some people are touchers. There are three reasons:

1. Both parents were touchers.

2. One parent was a toucher and had the most impact or handling for the first few years.

3. They were raised by surrogate parents who were touchers.

Touching wasn't the focus of many research projects until the mid 1980's, and the best studies have occurred in the last twenty years. One book, "Touch – The Human Significance" by Ashley Montague, 1984, is a wonderful book on the subject. To dramatize the importance of touch, I quote Gunilla Birkestad, a teacher who heads the 'School of Touch' in Sweden.[1] She has taught Tactiletherapists and Tactiltherapy in Sweden. On her website she recounts the following story.

I worked with a man diagnosed as a spastic epileptic and possibly autistic who had no speech or physical ability and his limbs were curled and twisted. I placed my hand on his shoulder and the other hand on his elbow. Fifteen minutes later the arm I was holding straightened. After I touched my hand to his hip and knee for fifteen minutes his leg straightened. Soon his entire body was normal.

The power of touch is, for the most part, unknown by most new mothers and fathers. Touching can convey anger, love, warmth, coldness, hostility etc. The absence of touch can be extremely detrimental, especially to newborns and young children.

Many insects and animals rely almost exclusively on tactile sensations to mate, reproduce, calm, and bond. This is true especially with bees, monkeys, apes and elephants.

---

1   To see more about Gunilla Birkestad, simply type in her name on the internet.

Based upon a lifelong study of this extremely important subject and analyzing its ramifications while coaching clients on this subject, I have concluded the following:

- Touchers almost NEVER become non-touchers

- Non-touchers rarely modify their non-touching behavior

- Touchers are happier, healthier, live longer and succeed more... usually

- Non-touchers usually marry non-touchers

- Non-touchers are less able to make changes in their lives

- Divorce is at a higher rate in marriages between non-touchers and touchers

- Human resource management almost always ignores this important subject

- Being totally aware you're a non-toucher 'can' help you be more of a toucher

- The subject is so personal...be extremely careful in talking about it

- The behavior of non-touchers is almost always self-restricting

- Non-touchers are more insecure...usually

- Non-touchers usually had at least one non-touching parent

- New born infants who receive little to no touching for an extended time WILL grow up as a non-toucher

After reading the points just listed, (if you are a non-toucher), you may now think you should be more of a toucher. I agree, but it is extremely difficult to change from a non-toucher to a toucher. BUT, you can begin becoming more of a toucher by touching your children or spouse more. Some people become more of a toucher by asking others in their home for a hug. People will give you a hug when you ask for it. This hug will be difficult, but it begins the road to becoming 'more' of a toucher. Be patient. It may take you years, but you will be happier. At the end of the chapter there are two anecdotes about how two non-touchers started touching more.

Touching can make or break a sale; make or break a relationship, disturb or enhance a friendship. Touching is always a healing, loving and improving, happier and better type of behavior.

Clearly, touching is extremely healthier for young babies and children. During wars many babies died from marasmus, meaning a wasting away or sometimes referred to today as 'failure-to-survive'. This syndrome was particularly seen in orphanages after World War II in Europe. The death rate of babies there was extremely high even though they were well fed and 'technically' very well cared for. The cause of so many infant deaths was determined to be from very little expressive touching mainly because the babies outnumbered the staff people.[2]

This author is a toucher and as a father, I was unaware of the importance of touching when my first son was born at only four pounds. He was incubated for several days. During this time he was rarely touched. Little did I or his mother know then that we had fixed his entire life as a non-toucher. This son will easily acknowledge that he is a 'non-toucher'. Of my five other children, all but this son is a toucher. All my children were held and lovingly touchced as infants and children, but none had the same medical isolation as my first son had.

The lack of touching in newborns and small children can produce:

- Weight losses; lack of weight gain
- Stunted growth; lack of appetite
- Lower body temperature; lower resistance to infection
- Apathy or regressing to the fetal stage

Sometimes the touching of siblings may help implant touching on these children. In some orphanages during wwii it was observed that when two siblings were together and touched more often their survival rate increased. This was in an orphanage which had few adults to care for these children.[3]

---

2   Nonverbal Communications, Randall P. Harrison, Michigan State University Press, 1974 P 119 Flora Davis writes, "A child will recognize NVS better as a child than as an adult."
3   Ibid, p. 119

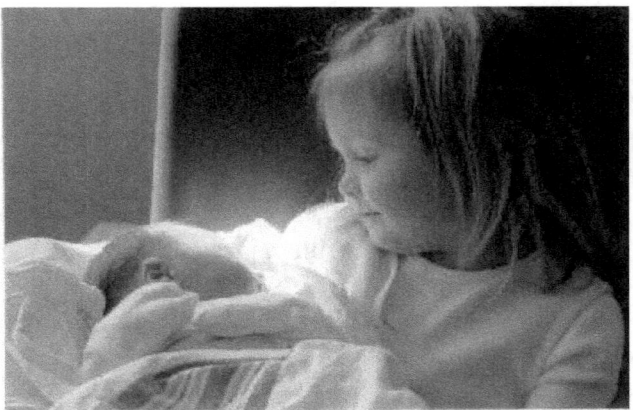

There is a great deal of research about siblings being raised without both parents who managed quite well because of their own interactive touching, playing and the occasional touching of adults. The adults around them also did not isolate the siblings.

I would like to add a personal observation. When a man or a woman becomes old and are placed in a hospital or nursing home, they still require tactile experiences because touching clearly has a healing affect. As a volunteer at several nursing homes, I have seen much evidence that older people who have visitors who hug and touch them, appear to be happier and may recover faster and prosper better than those who are abandoned by family. It's at both ends of life, very young and very old, touching and holding and a perceived caring has major therapeutic and recovery benefits, plus a happier child and patient.

FOUR ANECDOTES ABOUT
THE IMPORTANCE OF TOUCHING

LARRY: TOUCHING HEALS AND BONDS

At one of my two day seminars, I talked about the sensitive subject of touching. Before our class started on the second night, Larry asked if he could share a story with everyone. It turned out his story was extremely personal and made a big impact on everyone. He said he realized after our first session that he had never hugged Lily, his 16 year-old daughter. It was an astonishing discovery and one he couldn't get out of his mind. He said that Lily had never asked for him to give her a hug either. He said he concluded that she hadn't asked for a hug because she knew he did want to give it. He decided to make an effort to change that behavior.

This observation by a non-toucher is common, but most people consciously decide not to change anything. It's too difficult. Larry was an exception. When he asked my permission to tell the class about what happened after our first session the night before, he was already in tears. Larry set the scene. His wife sat at one end of the dining room table. At the other end was his chair. Lily sat on the long side of the table with her back facing the kitchen door.

After struggling with the thought that he was going to hug his daughter this particular night, Larry got up and walked behind Lily, BUT was unable to touch her.

He turned quickly and went into the kitchen where, with tears in his eyes, he gathered the strength to return to the dinning room table and stand behind Lily's chair. As he came up behind his daughter, his only decision was to place his hands on his daughter's shoulders, which he did. Immediately, Lily's right hand moved to her left shoulder and placed it on her father's hand. Then she tilted her head sideways and rested it against his hand. They both began crying…soon he said we were both out of control crying.

Slowly she stood up leaving her father's hand on her shoulder. Larry, with tears in his eyes, slowly and with great trepidation, gave his daughter a gentle, weak hug. Lily returned his weak hug with a bear hug. Larry's hug got stronger. Both continued crying.

Mother, still at the table, was dumfounded. She had no idea what was going on. She had never seen her husband hug their daughter. She got up and joined the hug as a threesome hug...a little awkward, but so was the moment. Mom asked over and over what the problem was. Did her husband do something? What was the problem? Finally, Larry said, "It's my problem. I realized last night that I had never hugged (his daughter)." Lily said, "Dad that was the first hug you ever gave me. Mom was now crying...all clinging together in one family hug.

Larry went on to say it was a very difficult moment for him. Larry came from a non-touching family. He had never seen his parents hug. They never hugged him and so hugging was not in his life,...ever!

Sometime later that night, after the hug, Lily said, "Dad, I knew you loved me, but...." Then there was silence. Both cried again and Larry said they hugged again. Larry had trouble talking about this first hug, but could already see a change in his daughter and maybe himself.

About five years later, I got a letter from Larry. I quote the last lines, "I sleep better and I like myself better. I actually need these hugs more than my daughter does. My wife says I seem happier. I am. I hug my daughter every time I see her which isn't often. I even hug my wife more too. Thanks for changing our lives...especially mine."

Larry is the one who changed their lives. I just got him to think about the subject. But, I do feel good inside for helping a family get closer. I get paid for my services, but there isn't enough money to equal those wonderful nonverbal rewards in my life.

Many people have been raised by non-touchers and the consequences of this kind of behavior in childhood are huge. If you're a non-toucher, try to become a toucher...slowly at first and I promise the fear and funny feelings you have in the beginning will slowly and gradually ease to some extent. An infrequent hugger is better than a non-hugger. Hug away.

KIM: THE CHALLENGE OF INITIATING THE FIRST HUG

In a Midwest town I worked with a large hospital counseling nurses. In the evening I held short seminars and after one of these Kim approached me crying. She stood silent for several seconds in front of me. I thought what could she possibly want. Maybe she was going to withdraw from my class. She had never said one word in over five hours of the seminars. She rarely looked at me and never took notes. She mainly looked at the other people. Then came the shocker. She told me she had never hugged her father and he was old and she wanted to hug him at least once in her life. Kim was a major non-toucher. She had all of the cluster signals: poor eye contact, head down when she talked, soft voice, angle posture, no gestures and even unconsciously would step back when she talked.

Kim was perhaps the template of the severe non-toucher. Sometimes I can guess what my seminar students will ask me; they give off signals which suggest those questions. I was floored by Kim's request. She was a severe non-toucher and chose never to want to change that.

"I have never hugged my father." Then she started crying and walked away. I decided not to follow her as I knew this was very difficult for her.

It was some time before she pulled herself together and came back… this time I made sure I was sitting. I am much taller than Kim and standing over her may have intimidated her. I deliberately lowered my position to the point where she now was slightly above me. This often gives some people an easier moment to say something which they deemed difficult.

She sat down and apologized for crying. My response was, "Is your father a non-toucher?" "Big one," she answered. " Can you help me?" I wanted to say I'll give it try, but Kim was a classical BIG non-toucher and it seemed to me I wouldn't be around long enough to make much headway with her.

We agreed to meet once a week for a half hour and see what happened. After we had met for about a month, I realized I was not going to be able to her help. Her traditions of not touching were insurmountable. We agreed to talk on the telephone once in a while. Nothing I said had any effect. I was convinced she would never hug her father.

On one telephone call about two months later, we both agreed it was a lost cause and to stop talking on the phone. Then, at that moment, I was prompted to say, "Kim, let's try something. When will you see your father again?"

"This weekend," she replied.

I suggested that after a few minutes of being with her father that she needed to walk up to him and say "Dad, I've had a bad day…I need a hug" and see what happens. Maybe he will show compassion for you and give you a hug. She didn't think she could do that, but nothing else had worked so I told her to try it.

Monday night she called me to say it worked and she and her father had hugged two more times during the weekend. I never heard from Kim again, but felt good I had that impression.

I decided that if Kim could hug a family member then there was hope for new counseling appointments. I have seen only a couple of others who were non touchers to the extinct that Kim projected. I believe Kim had the most severe case of the fear to touch others I've ever had.

The skin is the physical boundary of the human body and when touched accidentally or intentionally, the messages vary from pain to exaltation. It is a major receiver for all kinds of messages. Our culture's social relationships are learned through touch; the handshake, holding, kissing. Not everyone is a toucher. Americans are basically a low contact culture. The British are even less touchers. The Central and South Americans are major touchers.

When I visited a very good friend of mine in a nursing home, I discovered even more about skin-touching. The following anecdote speaks for itself.

Miss freyhoffr: it applies to the elderly, too!

Touching heals more arguments, feelings and wounds than all the medicine in the world.

Miss Freyhoffer was an elderly woman when I first met her. She was the first piano teacher at Michigan Agricultural College which became Michigan State University and loved by every pupil, friend, stranger and colleagues.

She never married and lived alone. When she was too old to walk unassisted, she happily ordered a walker. If someone asked Miss Freyhoffer if he or she could visit her at her apartment, would always say 'come for lunch'.

When you arrived she asked you to sit while (pushing her walker all over her small apartment) she would get the silverware and dishes "NO HELP THANK YOU!" she would yell when I offered to help. She continued to slide her walker around the room getting all these things she needed, first cook then to serve a wonderful lunch. For her silverware she would reach in a high box in her closet labeled 'Marilyn'. For some dishes she would get these from a lower box, labeled "Christine'. When she passed on, there would be no discussion what relative got what.

She was very thin and frail so most people felt uncomfortable in hugging her. Those who refrained from hugging her missed her major need…getting a hug. She always hugged you when you came in and insisted on getting a departing hug! This wonderful woman told me years earlier when she was about seventy. "I need a hug Ron…old people may need more hugging than young ones do."

Summary: most old people have skin hunger, meaning their skin becomes the stronger connector to friends and family when they are touched. Don't forget that.

GARY: TOUCHED EVERY SALES PROSPECT…AND GOT AWAY WITH IT

Gary is a real estate broker in the Midwest and may be one of the best sales people I have ever worked with. He attended one of my seminars and spent more time re-confirming everything I said than learning new skills. Gary was a 'natural born salesman'. Gary has one belief, which breaks every rule of touching and non-touching. And he does it all the time. What is amazing, he gets away with it.

Gary claims emphatically and without hesitation…Unless I touch the buyer/seller, who wants to list their home with me, and unless they touch me, I will not close the transaction. Whenever I have touched them and they have touched me, I make a deal. It NEVER fails me."

Having observed non-touchers for many years, I can accept his premise, but caution needs to emphasized here. Touching can be risky at best and worse at the wrong times. You can lose the magic moment in sales or negotiating. Gary agreed non-touchers are more difficult to close. Gary can recognize non-touchers. Here is his criteria and I can add very little to it.

Says Gary, "Non-touchers have weak eye contact...they rarely look at you...usually they are soft spoken...with very few gestures...usually they have a low voice... and they don't have much of a sense of humor." But I love them and I guess they can see that.

I often say, Right on...Gary nailed it. I add that non-touchers do not cope with life as well as touchers either, usually. They have more health problems and, as a rule, they are not as happy as touchers. There are plenty of examples that they are also more insecure.

THE TOUCHING PROFILE

RATE YOUR TOUCHING BEHAVIOR

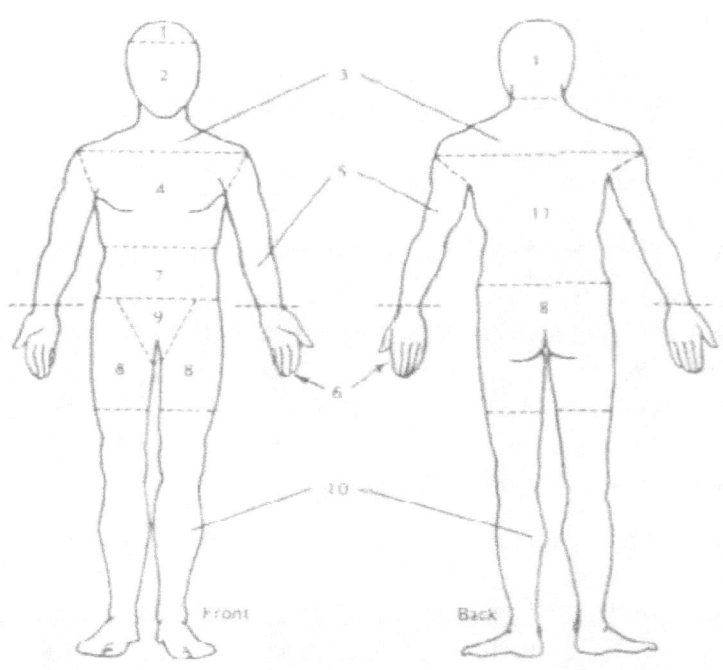

There are eleven different zones of the drawing of the human body. To determine if you are an active toucher or an inactive toucher, add each of the numbers from zones where you have been touched (or done the touching), and see how your touching changes from person to person.

Count them for both category 1 and 2, then look at how you rate as a toucher or a non-toucher.

1. Add up each of the zones that you have touched on your:

    A) children _____

    B) spouse _____

    C) mother _____

    D) father _____

    E) best male friend _____

    F) best female friend _____

2. Add up each of the zones that you have been touched by your:

    A) children _____

    B) spouse _____

    C) mother) _____

    D) father _____

    E) best male friend _____

    F) best female friend _____

Results of Touching Profile: Major, healthy toucher 40 - 50, Moderate toucher 30 - 39, Weak toucher 20 - 29, Not a toucher 0 -19. This is an unscientific test and is intended to give you an indication ONLY. Most people know they are touchers or not and usually to what degree. If you fall below 30 you need to think about becoming more of a toucher. It is believed by many sociologists and other professionals in the business of helping people with behavioral problems, that the more of a toucher you are the happier and healthier you should be. This writer believes the more you are a toucher, the better you can cope with life and the longer you may have good health. Touchers are outgoing and often loud and active talkers. Non touchers are usually quiet spoken, have fewer gestures and expressions and laugh less. Non touchers don't like to be the center of attention. Big touchers love to be the center of attention.

CHAPTER 19

RARE - EYE CONTACT PEOPLE

SOME PEOPLE CAN'T LOOK YOU IN THE EYE

When teaching my nonverbal classes, I usually make the comment, "Some of us are afraid of strangers' eyes because we don't love them enough." Almost always a student will ask "What do you mean we don't love them enough?" My answer is, "When you care about the person you are talking with, who manifests rare eye-contact, it will be difficult for them if you give long moments of direct eye contact." So for these people, give less eye contact back. Reduce the number of times you look straight into their eyes.

Rare eye contact creates problems of communication for many adults. Some people often say, "I can't stand anybody who can't look me in the eye." It is well documented that rare eye contact people have lower self esteem. People who offer little to no direct eye contact are almost always less secure than those who give more eye contact. Rare eye contact in small children may have to do with some emotional problems. As a parent, it would be wise to mention this to your doctor.

When children are not given much eye-to-eye contact by their parents, their verbal messaging may be much weaker. A child knows something is very important when Mom or Dad stops and holds them to look them straight into their eyes. Mom's message seems extra important at that moment.

If you are somewhat insecure, you might try giving more eye contact to everyone you meet. This consultant has helped some to overcome their fears and anxiety by encouraging them to give longer eye contact with people. It is difficult to do, but if you are one who hates to look people in the eye, try it. For some of my clients, it has had good results. It may take you a long time to increase eye contact, but it will have positive results. Not looking at someone when speaking to them draws attention to the behavior. Most people expect others to look at them when they are engaged in conversation.

If we realize that many people with poor eye contact are a little scared to give it, perhaps we can ignore our requirement for more of it. As I say to my clients. "To understand is to forgive."

TWO ANECDOTES ABOUT POOR EYE CONTACT FROM MY ONE-ON-ONE COACHING

KAREN: WAS OKAY, BUT HER HUSBAND WASN'T

Professor Karen was a colleague at a university where I taught non-verbal communication, drama/mime and rhetoric for almost five years. She taught composition and invited me to her classes occasionally to lecture on dialogue for novels and short stories. We became close friends on a professional level and spent some time together correcting mutual student papers in our cafeteria.

One of our students wrote a paper about her problem of never finding a husband or steady date. It was an excellent paper and triggered Karen to talk to me about her fear she would not find a husband either. Karen was very pretty and articulate yet she did not have a boyfriend and it really bothered her. When she told me this I was surprised. She asked me what I thought about her problem and could my expertise in non-verbal communication help her. I basically deflected any involvement in the issue. I was not prepared at that time to address her nonverbal question. She said she knew she had some signals which were wrong and wanted my help. I agreed that someday we would talk.

One of her negative nonverbal problems was poor eye contact. In the cafeteria when we had a one-on-one conversation she constantly was looking around the room as she talked seemingly looking for someone. When we shared student conversations and writing, her eye contact was basically on everything else in the room except what we were talking about.

The other negative signal was that she never stopped talking. Nearly anything could distract her from her intended tasks. This is likely a trait connected to her tradition, one passed from parents. I decided to refrain from mentioning it. Traditional behavior from parents is extremely difficult to change and sometimes painful to discuss. She asked me again and again for our little chat about her nonverbal signals. The day finally came.

We talked for about fifteen minutes and she was totally unaware of both of her negative nonverbal behaviors - poor eye contact and constantly talking. I mentioned both of these behaviors. She made excuses for these behaviors and was convinced it was not a problem she needed to work on. A typical first response and one I expected.

About two months later, Karen approached me in the hallway of our administration building, saying, "I have to talk to you as soon as possible." We went to her office and she told me about a date she was had and caught herself talking for most of that date. I told her that was a great moment for her. Now she knew she did talk a lot and maybe she could change that habit. She also told me that she caught herself looking everywhere and not at the person she had a date with.

She told me this with tears in her eyes. This catharsis was heavy on her. It is very common for a person who discovers a negative signal they didn't know they had to overreact and beat them self up. Almost always my clients believe, if I saw their nonverbal signals, everyone else saw them too. I told her not everyone sees what a nonverbalist sees, even though I know many people see negative nonverbal signals and soon ignore them or get new friends.

To discover your negative signals is the first part of changing or modifying them. Most people never change their nonverbal signals, they are too ingrained in their subconsciousness.

Before I left this university, Karen called to tell me was engaged. She says she still looks all over the rooms she's in, but has reduced her talking… (her words) a little. She said that when she met her fiancée she deliberately 'didn't talk' and was so quiet that he asked her several times if she was okay. She also said, "Once I hooked him I started talking all the time again, but you know what, he still loves me. He's not a talker anyway and he's totally disinterested in what other people are doing or saying. We're a good match." Traditions never go away.

U.S. CUSTOMS: WHERE RARE EYE CONTACT REALLY MATTERS

Nonverbal signals sort out people who are carrying something they don't want found.

The Chicago US Customs contacted me to assist in training agents for spotting passengers carrying contraband at O'Hare International Airport. This was in 1974. If I could provide enough evidence that nonverbal training would be valuable for their agents, then possibly a national program of this kind of training might be implemented. The test period was to be for two weeks.

Every arriving passenger had to enter a secured area where there were at least five tables with agents prepared to determine if contraband or any illegal items could be identified. There were several agents working both sides of the passenger's clearance tables, but most were on the exit side of the tables. My assignment was to signal the agent nearest to me when I saw some nonverbal signals which triggered suspicion. For obvious reasons, I will not mention the signals I looked for. I would always walk back and forth outside the lines as this gave me a longer view of each passenger.

For the first three hours, nothing unusually appeared. Then just before we were going to dinner, a short woman in a mink coat who looked like everybody's grandmother type had a signal which bothered me. I admit this woman just didn't look like someone trying to sneak something across the borders. When I signaled the agent to check her out, they looked dumfounded. I was pointing out a woman who seemed thoroughly harmless, the least likely profile for someone trying to bring in undeclared items. They hesitated, but decided to check her out. I was a little nervous because this woman only had one nonverbal signal (no cluster) which caused me concern.

My first selection that day turned out positive. The grandmother had tried to sneak through customs an enormous amount of cash. I felt sorry for her when she started crying hysterically.

The most interesting subject was a young, tall, skinny man, maybe in his 30's. It was summertime and he was wearing silk shorts and a tank top and was carrying a small, grocery-like plastic bag with almost nothing in it. He also wore flip flops. He was almost naked ...AND, he had no luggage. How could he possibly be hiding anything?

He had many negative signals, so I signaled the agents. This young man had flown from Thailand to Chicago with no baggage, except this small plastic bag. The agents talked to him, then took him to an enclosed room nearby and questioned him further. Then they released him. All of the agents agreed with me this man had bad vibes and odd answers to their questions. But, he had nothing. He couldn't have anything.

The agents let him go. However, one of the agents decided he would watch the young man exit the building, as the outside windows permitted a view of this man from our second story location. He could see the exit door to the sidewalk and curb. The only place they could not see him was on the stairs descending from where we were.

Almost at the same moment our suspect exited to the street, a black luxury sedan pulled up and stopped. A very well dressed man jumped out of the driver's seat and popped the trunk where our suspect threw in his plastic bag. They both jumped into the car and started off. The agent who had followed, signaled an agent on the street ahead to stop the car and bring these two people back to the airport.

Suffice it to say after another interview of the suspect and a conversation with the well dressed man, they were brought inside and after 45 minutes of more examining, found the contraband. I leave it to the reader's imagination to make the correct conclusions to where he had hidden the illegal substance.

Training TSA agents at airports to spot unusual behaviors has been a strong requirement since September 11, 2001, and training of these agents has been very intense and very sophisticated.

CHAPTER 20

HOW TO ASSIST PEOPLE WITH POOR EYE CONTACT

MIRRORING TO GET EYE CONTACT

When you are with a poor eye contact person, it is very difficult for effective verbal communication. This writer has been in many one-on-one conversations where there was little to no eye contact. I have actually solved that problem many times to improve eye contact. Here's how. I mirror back their eye contact moments. I give short glances staying on the other person's eye for a couple of seconds only…moving quickly off their eyes before the other person looks into my eye. In other words, when they look into my eye, I move off quickly before they do, which allows them to stay on my eye longer. In a few moments, I will glance back to see if they are still on my eye. If they are, I will move off fairly quickly.

Most people probably want to look others in the eye, but for some people it is very difficult. When I am not looking directly at their eyes, they are more comfortable to make eye contact. I will continue giving quick and brief looks to one of their eyes, each time getting off this eye connection before they do. This intermittent locking on and off of their eyes relaxes the other person. They now don't see long eye contact from me. Their problem is lessened.

Believe it or not, after this little gymnastic eye game, the rare eye contact person begins to hold their eyes on me longer…UNTIL they seem okay looking at me for a few minutes at a time. I basically have maneuvered them in to more eye contact without their knowledge. This improves communication! Usually, from that moment on, there is more substantive communication between us. I should add usually, even though I have increased their eye contact with me, they will not stay locked on my eyes too long. Rare eye contact people can't stay too long on anyone staring at their eyes. However, more eye contact produces warmer relationships.

Little eye contact *never* occurs when a flirtation and mutual interest are at play. The eye contact then is greater to say the least, even from people who rarely give it.

This author has used mirroring eye contact behavior many times with success. What you are actually doing is transferring the prospect's behavior of poor eye contact to yourself. Another way of saying this is, it transfers the anxiety from them to you. To them, you may seem a little insecure and also they understand this feeling. This lightens their concerns and increases better communication. Try it–because it works.

CHAPTER 21

EIGHTEEN NONVERBAL SIGNALS YOU CAN TAKE TO THE BANK

It is with great confidence, working in this field for nearly 40 years that I make the following list.

The following eighteen nonverbal signals almost always have a true meaning every time you see them. It is amazing that of the hundreds of nonverbal signals or messages without words, there are so few this author believes you can rely on as being true with indisputable meanings every time you see them.

The discipline of recognizing nonverbal signals seems, to this consultant, is a skill you are born with and at various levels of abilities. Clearly, I was given this special insight. I have met very few people in my lifetime who also have a special skill to recognize most of the nonverbal signals. It is startling for this consultant to have met less than five people in my lifetime that, when I demonstrate the signal or just show them a picture of a signal, they have identified them correctly.

It seems some of my children and grandchildren have this skill of measuring people's body signals and I believe genetics is the reasons why they seem to have this skill. It reminds me of a concert pianist coach I know who said, "I can teach everyone to play the piano, but I can count on one hand those whom I have been able to train to become a concert pianist of significant skills." The great pianist is born with something which, when given some direction and training become highly skilled musicians.

The following eleven nonverbal signals you can take to the bank depending upon when you see them and in context with spoken words. I should mention that some of these signals come ONLY in clusters and seeing the cluster is also a special gift. Fact! Some people can see cluster signals and some cannot. I have rarely been able to train a person to see a nonverbal cluster. If this book makes you aware that some signals are communicated in clusters, it will have a significant value for you. Start looking for clusters and your skill to read many of these signals will increase.

These eighteen nonverbal signals which, when seen, you can depend upon the meaning stated here. I also acknowledge that there are other signals in clusters which I have not named here. Those signals are also in clusters and are so subtle when given, it is nearly impossible to see. So, I offer the more obvious ones.

Remember, seeing a nonverbal signal gives you communication power, if only to say to yourself, "That signal could have meant such-in-such." That is communication power! So let me name the eleven signals which I believe are true every time I see them.

1 TAKING A BREATH FROM THE MOUTH

While you are talking to another person and you see this person take a breath through their mouth STOP talking immediately. They have taken a breath through their mouth for ONLY TWO reasons: ONE, to take a DRINK. It is impossible to swallow without taking a breath first. The second reason a person takes a breath through their mouth and NOT their nose is TO SPEAK.

It could be the most critical moment in a two-way conversation. When you see someone taking a breath from their mouth STOP talking and ask, "Did you have a question?" Or, "Did you want to say something?" Learn to see this unique signal and your communication effectiveness will improve substantially. Improving your communication helps your entire life in every relationship.

2 PLACING ONE FINGER, SEVERAL FINGERS OR PALM OVER THE MOUTH WHILE TALKING

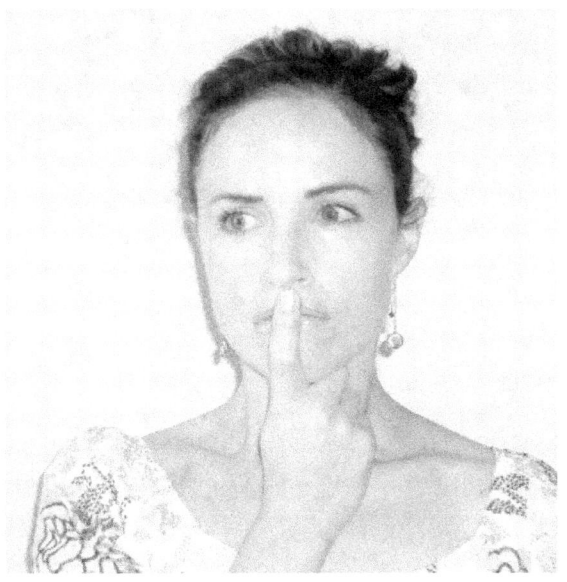

Placing the index finger over the mouth *while* talking has one meaning: the person speaking is very insecure about what they are saying…even believing they shouldn't say it. So, when you see this signal you have two choices. One is to realize the person is insecure about what they are saying and possibly take advantage of the moment and dominate or control the conversation. The other reaction you can take is to soften your nonverbal signals in a way of approval and acceptance toward the insecure person. Try to say and DO things to remove their insecurity.

If you do this, their insecurity is placated and often this person becomes less insecure at that moment. Reducing or eliminating all of your nonverbal signals which convey 'dominance and control' is one thing you can do. You can also lower your voice volume and speak slower. You can also try to be less visible by dropping your head with less eye contact. You can use fewer gestures and do less body movements on your part. I have used these methods successfully. You can also agree with their comments even if you silently disagree. All these suggestions will help the other person be more comfortable and improve communication effectiveness.

It is also very common to see several fingers over the mouth while they are speaking. Both one finger and several fingers indicate insecurity.

Often a person will place their entire palm over their mouth…all three of these gestures are signals of a degree of insecurity. Again, reduce all signals of your dominance and control and be more forgiving and this will placate these negative feelings.

ONE ANECDOTE ABOUT SIGNALS OF INSECURITY

GWEN: *ALWAYS HAD FINGERS OVER HER MOUTH WHEN SHE TALKED*

As you just read, placing the finger or fingers over the mouth while talking has a major nonverbal message. Not many people do this, but Gwen did it every time she talked. Few notice this seemingly inconsequential gesture. My mother placed her finger or palm over her mouth when she talked almost every time.

This gesture is one of six, when you see it, that has an indisputable message - this person is insecure. I must add that most people are insecure...about something.

People have phobias which come to the surface with some settings, which turn their particular phobia on. Everyone has a soft spot on their security blanket and when this spot is triggered by a word, gesture, sound or even an apparent meaning hitting at this soft spot, they get anxious, move about more...walk away, bend backwards, turn to an angle or contort their face and frequently cover their mouth while talking.

Many things can hit these soft spots of insecurity. The doubting of yourself is your worse enemy. Your doubt, worry or anything which threatens to puncture your insecurity blanket can negatively change your communication, a positive countenance and at times your life.

Remember, placing the finger, fingers or even the palm over the mouth while talking is a clear signal of doubt or insecurity.

3 THE AGREEMENT AND DISAGREEMENT OF THE DOWN GESTURE

AGREEMENT

The down gesture is the downward movement of a body part or parts. As a nonverbal gesture, the significant aspect of the down gesture is normally done to validate or approve something. For instance, the down gesture of a clinched fist to a table top typically indicates that the person is validating the truth of what he or she is saying. It is a gesture of positive emphasis. This down gesture when used in agreement with someone's comments is done in a cluster of signals which include the head up, excellent eye contact and usually a pleasant countenance.

THE DOWN GESTURE USED WITH THE SPOKEN WORDS, "I DON'T KNOW!"

DISAGREEMENT

This same down gesture becomes a disagreement message when the same cluster of signals are used as the person is speaking the phrase, "I don't know." This cluster signal includes the fist hitting the table top, but now the eye contact is OFF the others at the table. The head moves down so the face is more hidden. This cluster is now in disagreement and the person IS lying! You can take it to the bank.

For this author, the cluster of three signals of the arm, hand and head moving at the same time, while the person says, "I don't know" has a very significant message! All of this action happens very fast.

Every time I have seen this cluster with the denial, the person drops his head so his face, and particularly his eyes, are NOT seen by anyone. It is often a jarring interruption at a meeting because the movement is strong and the voice is usually loud.

Again, this cluster connected with the spoken words, "I don't know," is a lie.

I have included two anecdotes about this cluster. The first time I saw it was when I was much younger and wasn't as secure telling my client that his own, high priced lawyer was lying. I sweated that experience out for several days and was finally vindicated.

This cluster of signals I have seen less than ten times in all the years I have been working as a nonverbal consultant.

This gesture includes the arm and hand moving from a higher position down toward the desk.

This cluster shows the hand about to slam on the desk while the person says, "I don't know."

WHEN YOU DON'T KNOW
ALL YOUR SIGNALS GO UP!

When someone doesn't know, EVERY gesture, head movement and facial expressions will GO UP! They **NEVER** go down! When someone is convinced that he/she doesn't know, their nonverbal signals will go up by raising eyebrows, hands, arms, head and shoulders and most of the time the eyes will dart upward for an instant, and then depending upon the skill of the liar, return to the other person they are in disagreement with.

In the anecdotes that follows, I offer two examples of nonverbal messages which clearly 'say' I don't know. Notice the signals are usually upwards.

Also notice how subtle these signals are and most of the message is in the face, which liars will hide when in disagreement.

TWO ANECDOTES ON THE DOWN GESTURE WHILE SPEAKING "I DON'T KNOW!"

*C*ARLOS: *THE MILLION DOLLAR GESTURE*

Pictured here is Carlos Piaget and the author

Carlos was a close friend who was born in Peru of Swiss parents and raised all over South America and Europe. At 28 years of age, he had put together a business plan for the first shopping center in Switzerland. Carlos had assembled investors for a pre-deal signing meeting at a Geneva bank. Eight people would be at a major bank's conference room. Germany, Switzerland, France, Belgium and Liechtenstein were represented along with Carlos' lawyer from New York. Carlos was well aware of my nonverbal counseling and invited me to sit in on this meeting. I would not sit at the table, but in a chair next to the wall where I could see everyone. I was introduced as a marketing consultant from America and was there to join everyone for lunch.

The president of the bank spent the entire morning getting to know each of the men at the table. Carlos' lawyer, and to some extent, everyone else was anxious to get the meeting started rather than 'who are you and what have you done'. The bank president had actually accomplished an amazing thing. He knew a great deal about everyone at the meeting and knew their possible strengths and weaknesses. The bank president also knew who was going to be power player, be reticent, and who would follow easily. These introductions took the entire morning. It was now time for lunch. A waitress came in and handed all of us menus and took our orders for lunch.

After a lengthy lunch the meeting resumed and after a short time most of us were ready for a nap. The meeting was going very well until… Carlos' own New York lawyer responding to a question directed to him, replied "I don't know." As he pounded his fist on the table, (a down gesture), I was startled. I had just seen a nonverbal gesture contradict a verbal statement. Did I just see Carols' lawyer lie to everyone including Carlos? I was positive I had, but my mind was thinking, 'no that's Carlos' lawyer…he would not lie to him.' But he did!

A meeting was scheduled for the following Tuesday at a different bank for presenting a letter of credit and signing a document to fund the 'first' shopping center in Switzerland. The only people who needed to be there were Carlos, his lawyer and two of the other lawyers. The meeting was set for Tuesday at 2 P.M. We all parted company and headed back to Carlos' office in Neuchatel one hour away.

Before we left, Carlos was able to get me aside and ask if everything was okay. I said, "No."

"What is wrong?" he asked.

I said, "I will tell you later."

I refused to say anything until Carlos' lawyer had left for the airport. Finally, Carlos asked again. What I was about to say bothered me greatly and, for a few moments, I doubted my own observations. I was about to say that Carlos was paying for a high-priced New York lawyer, who was maneuvering to take the whole thing himself by not showing up at the Tuesday meeting. If I was right, Carlos would lose the 750,000 Swiss francs funding ($1,000,000 U.S.). If I was wrong, my advice could severely damage the entire transaction on Tuesday, and jeopardize Carlos' participation in the deal.

Again, Carlos asked me what was bothering me. I told him that I wanted to think about it. He told me that since he was paying me for my services I was obligated to tell him what I knew. When someone makes a closed statement such as an emphatic 'I don't know' they will always gesture up...not down! An up gesture; hands up, eye brows up, arms up or all of these at the same time...they are thinking or in this case, saying "I don't know. Carlos' attorney had said no as he gestured or pounded table down." Carlos looked at me in silence for along time, then said, "So?" When your lawyer said "I don't know", he pounded the desk...with a down gesture." Carlos still looked puzzled and said, "So?" I had a very difficult time responding. He repeated his, "So?

"So," I said, "He's lying." There was a very long pause, and then Carlos sat down. After another long pause Carlos asked, "Ron, are you sure?" Before I could respond, he said, "If you're wrong I could lose this deal."

I said I knew that. Then I said, "But if I am right you can get this whole deal all by yourself. Your lawyer is supposed to be bringing a letter of credit. One of you are going to get this funding... alone, either you or your lawyer."

One nonverbal signal conflicting with a verbal statement stood between Carlos acquiring or losing the funding for the first shopping center in Switzerland. I told Carlos several times to get his own letter of credit and show up on Tuesday...he would be alone. All this happened on a Thursday afternoon and my plane back to the states was the next morning.

Upon my arrival back home Carlos kept calling me about every three hours. I told him to stop calling until Monday night and I would give him my final answer. I didn't think lightly about my answer, but I knew what I knew and I trusted what I knew; a down gestures DOES NOT confirm a doubt or question. His lawyer was lying, period! His motive was unclear, but not his truthfulness.

On Monday night I told Carlos to show up the next day with his letter of credit...his lawyer wasn't showing. I must admit Tuesday was a worrisome day for me. I knew what I knew, but did I really see that gesture? Yes I did….so I waited…all day it seemed. There was six hours difference in time zones, so after eight in the evening I sat by the phone. Carlos called me at 11:30 P.M.. His lawyer did not show with his letter of credit. Carlos did. It required new documents to be typed up and cleared.

The following day Carlos' lawyer showed up at the bank. He was surprised about what had happened the previous day. He was even more surprised that Carlos had successfully obtained a letter of credit and the initial agreement for funding the project. After his lawyer left the banker's office, the banker called Carlos and told him what had just happened and that he was sure his lawyer was on his way to see him.

Carlos called me and asked what he should do. I flippantly said, "Buy him a drink and tell him about nonverbal communication." He bought him a drink, but chose not to tell him about me. His lawyer apologized eventually and they were friends for many years afterwards. Some nonverbal signals can be more important than verbal messages.

THE MILLION DOLLAR GESTURE

TOM: HEAD MOVEMENT WAS EITHER A CONTRADICTION OR A CONFIRMATION…BUT WHICH?

A friend of mine and I had been asked to produce an industrial film for a major retailer in Chicago. We needed to know the budget before we created a first draft of the script. Without a budget figure we were at a major disadvantage for both us and our client. So we set an appointment in one of the upper floors of the Sears Tower in Chicago. We had our appointment with the decision maker and we knew it by placement and size – corner office and large. Our meeting seemed to come apart when we got to the subject of the budget.

The executive talked around the budget, but gave us no clear dollar range. He wanted a great deal, but kept saying, "I don't know if we can afford this or that." We asked if he knew the budget that had been allocated. He paused, looked at some papers then said "No!" BUT… when he said 'no', he dropped his head down similar to those head movements which accompany a verbal 'yes'. In other words, his head moved down quickly then bounced up again. That's how people usually say 'yes'. I was confused. I thought he was foxy…then he slammed his open hand on his desk and said, "I'd like to give you a figure, but don't have it yet. Could you do it under (he mentioned a price)?" By slamming his open hand down on the table along with saying he didn't have a budget yet was all the info I needed. I said, "Let us work out a shooting schedule and get back to you with a figure.'

That relaxed him very much. I signaled my friend Jack to end the meeting, but he didn't know what I knew and kept seeking a more precise figure for their budget. I ended the meeting by standing up. Everyone stood up, shook hands and we left. My friend was upset by ending the meeting and told me so. I said, "I know his budget…at least I know what he wants to spend."

Reminder: when a person doesn't know, or there is any doubt or questions, all of the signals go UP!

We came in at twenty percent above his highest figure among many potential lower ones. We signed a contract to produce the film. When we were screening our film for the client, this man privately turned to me and said, "You knew I knew the budget didn't you?" I answered, "Pretty sure" knowing that my answer softened any perceived arrogance on my part. He asked me, "How did you know that?" Since by now we had a very good relationship, I told him about his head signal. He was fascinated and asked me to give my seminar to his sales people in the future (which I did). We became very good friends.

4 GROOMING GESTURES

Grooming gestures nearly always mean a fairly high degree of insecurity. The depth of that insecurity, according to this observer, cannot be quantified.

The most interesting example for me happened at NBC Television studios in New York City when I was in the control room of Studio 8H where the director and engineers rehearsed and broadcast the "Tonight Show" starring Johnny Carson. Before that interesting story, here are a few examples of grooming by men.

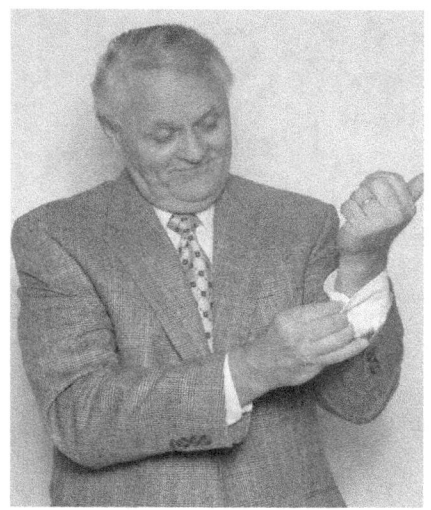

Grooming hair, cuff links, face, finger nails, wiping the face and inspecting or cleaning their finger nails are obvious grooming gestures.

JOHNNY CARSON: MAJOR INSECURITY, BUT ALMOST NOBODY SAW IT

Grooming gestures most often mean insecurity.

Dick Carson, Johnny's brother was a good friend of mine in the late 60's when he was the director of his brother's show, NBC's Tonight Show. Routinely I would go to the control room where Dick directed the cameras and commercial breaks at the studio in the Rockefeller Plaza building for the rehearsal and tape delayed show. I thought the rehearsals were more interesting than the broadcasts. Johnny had the strict policy of never appearing nor talking to any guest until he appeared in front of the audience. This kept all of his interviews fresh and spontaneous.

After rehearsals on some occasions, Dick and I would go to dinner. Dick would return to the studio and direct the show and I would go to my apartment. One evening Dick convinced me I should come back to the studio control room and watch the show as Johnny had a bit of business which I would enjoy.

When Johnny walked out through the curtains for his monologue, he began immediately to groom himself - fixing his tie, pulling his shirt-sleeves down, adjusting his cuff links, combing his hair with his hands and many other minor grooming gestures. Grooming gestures most often supports some kind of insecurity.

Johnny would also (when embarrassed or jarred out of his prepared monologue) snap his head sideways and stare at any technician or person nearby and lock in on that person while he silently stared….waiting for the laughter to subside, then whip his head back, move his eyes back and forth quickly. The audience found these nonverbal movements extremely funny while Johnny was trying to think of a funny line to continue. Most of the time he found one. All of these grooming gestures and quirky moves were silence yelling to a nonverbalist, "I am very insecure".

I was surprised Johnny Carson was insecure. He seemed so in control every night. Nevertheless, he had many nonverbal signals, which loudly spoke 'insecurity'. After the show I said to Dick, "I didn't know your brother was so insecure." Dick nearly jumped out of his chair and responded, "Insecure? He's the most insecure human being on this planet." Then Dick would site personal stories validating his comments.

Grooming gestures that suggest insecurity are mainly done by successful, well dressed people, but especially by those in the limelight or in the public's eye.

Having been around television performers on CBS and NBC a great deal of time in the late 50's and mid 70's, I can report that most comedians are very insecure and many have the grooming gestures.

Comics use humor and self-effacing humor to cover, hide and protect their insecurities. When you think about the history of the Jewish people, it is easy to understand why so many became the great comedians of the world; to mask their sadness and tortured past. So often the Jews who suffered or had families who suffered had great sadness and pain in their music, art, sculpture and books for many years. Then they turn these pains into creative and funny words, paintings and songs to make people happy, laugh, love and sing.

When I have interviewed a comic in his dressing room after keeping an audience in stitches for nearly two hours, they are almost all mute and very unfunny; almost depressing. Most of these great comics are quiet off stage and carrying a great deal of baggage. Henny Youngman is a great example. Yet on the stage, they transform themselves. They can get out of their past and with great skill gain great composure and power and are gifted entertainers.

5 THE PALM DOWN HANDSHAKE FOR MEN

In counseling Human Relation Directors at various corporations, I have heard several stories of men (women simply don't do it) who use the palm down handshakes. Every case I have heard about proved that a palm down handshake meant a high self image or a very strong ego. This section will add other handshakes as well as the down one.

The typical, non-threatening hand shake shown in the picture is the normal one used by men and most women.

As the palm turns down we begin to learn something which might be helpful in understanding this person.

As the palm of the hand turns down the self image of this person rises.

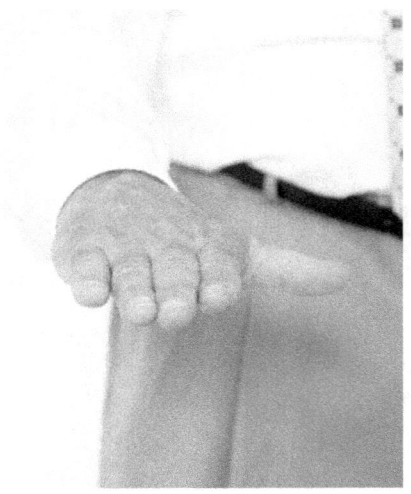

Here is the flat, palm down handshake. This person has an enormous self image. Sales companies want good egos in most of their executives, but the flat, totally turned down handshake is most likely from a man who is not much fun to work with or for. Several Human Relations Directors have learned this the hard way.

6 THE POLITICAL HANDSHAKE

I add this signal to those you can take to the bank as it is very often expected when shaking hands with a politician. This is especially true when the politician is alone or nearly alone with a possible supporter. In tight crowds this handshake is more difficult. While shaking hands the politician will often grab the back of the same arm and pull it closer in an unconscious attempt to pull this prospective 'vote' into his camp. It is so common.

7 THE 'I WANT SOMETHING' HANDSHAKE

Here a man (women almost never do it) shakes the hand while he grabs the top of the other shoulder and pulls it forward. The nonverbal message is this man 'wants something' and he is going to use all of his verbal skills and charm to get it. It doesn't mean a negative motive. It often is a positive desire to be close, to bond faster. But, pulling the other person in connects to his desire for wanting something.

8 THE MINISTER'S HAND SHAKE

Here is a hand shake that, for the most part, is only given by a pastor, minister or person of the cloth. Almost simultaneously, as they grab the right hand to shake, they will place their left palm gently over the hand shake covering it. The minister rarely will give a tight hand shake. Almost always, their head will be lowered and possibly tilted. Their voice will be softer usually. When this author has been given this handshake, frequently I will ask if they are a minister. Usually they confirm they have been.

9 THE FIVE GESTURES OF STOP!

(1) If you see this gesture it is clearly to stop. Stop talking. Stop interrupting. Stop something. There is no doubt about it, but we usually

don't do this gesture in normal conversations. It can be seen as a rude message. So, we usually start by giving a more subtle stop sign signal as you will see in the following photographs. This signal is almost never seen, but it clearly means 'to stop'.

(2) Then there is a more subtle signal to stop. Here both hands are up and out to the side and almost always with no eye contact To add emphasis to our subtle stop gesture, the person will turn his or her head away from the other person.

(3) Here's another less provocative stop sign. The palm is still forward, but lowered and placed to the side. There may or may not be eye contact, but they want you to stop talking. All of these changes to soften the full stop sign signal as shown in the first picture. Often, the other

hand is placed on the hip to draw attention to our gesture message. Most people miss this sign and keep talking.

(4) Often, people may place both palms out or to the side to lessen the powerful signal of 'stop talking'. They usually drop their head and disconnect their eye contact. They want the other person to stop, but don't want to give a 'loud' message so they will offer a 'softer' gesture, one that is not so obvious. However, most people don't see these subtle 'stop talking' signs.

(5) Probably the most subtle stop sign we can make is when we place only one finger outward, the fleshy part, facing forward as we do with the palm. Again, no eye contact. Nothing can be more subtle than this,

but it is the same message. This gesture usually is not seen. Isn't it amazing to know that there are an array of stop gestures?

10 THE SECRET MESSAGE OF A HAPPY FACE AND THE INDEX FINGER

As we have seen, a single finger to the side represents a very subtle sign of 'stop'. But when we place our index finger in front of us with the hand lower, plus the signal of a good countenance, this is a different message. It means we want to touch you, to let you know that the other person has been accepted…that we like this person. Touching is the greatest sign of love and friendship. It is a compliment.

11 BOTH HANDS ON THEIR CHEST

When you see this gesture by another person, it means the person is thinking, "Who me?" "Did I say that?" This sign clearly says that the listener is questioning or, for some reason doubting the message just heard. When you see this message, stop talking and ask, "Did you have a comment?" They will almost every time, respond with something contrary to what they just heard.

12 THREE GESTURES OF NOT UNDERSTANDING
FINGER(S) OR PALM OVER THE EYE

By now, you should recognize that the fingers of the hand play a major role in communicating messages to others. The hand and especially the fingers are so important to our daily lives. Isaac Newton said, "I know there is a God every time I see my thumb."

It is fascinating to this consultant how many nonverbal messages are conveyed by the hand, one finger or several fingers. If a person blocks their vision in one eye as they close the other eye *and* raise their head upwards while rubbing the eye, it means they 'can't see what you are saying". Stop talking and ask if they understood what you just said.

If they are rubbing their eye and their head down it can mean they don't understand or their eye itches. With either head position, you would be wise to ask, "Did you understand what I just said?" Here are three photos - one with one finger over the eye – the next with several fingers over their eye and lastly the palm hiding the eye. All these signals covering the eye while talking are signals of confusion.

It is the same message when they place their palm over one eye with their head up.

13 FLIPPED HANDS UP AND BACK OVER SHOULDERS

Here are clusters of gestures which should say to you the person you are talking to has surrendered or given up. Both hands go up and back over the shoulders. The person usually leans backwards as their head tilts backwards also. It is all of these signals in one fluid movement. Immediately, the person who gave this signal resumes their normal look. They would be thinking, "You win, I won't argue with you any more." Some add an expression which implies - "Have it your way." This one signal of raising both arms up high means the same thing all over the world - surrender.

14 STEEPLING THE HANDS LOW AND HIGH

Steepling is a signal which almost every time has a correct interpretation. This signal represents dominance, control, and ego which someone like O'Reilly must have to be so successful! Steepling almost always means a high or extremely high ego. Fox News' Bill O'Reilly steeples nearly every show even though he keeps his steepling low away from his face. The first photo (below left) shows a less powerful steepling signal. The ego here is less than the following pictures indicate. Notice as the steepling rises so does the ego.

It is very common for a person steepling to start low and gradually moves upwards until it nearly covers his/her face. For some hiding most of the face is a must!

The steepling here is higher; and so is the ego.

The interpretations of the preceding nonverbal steepling signals are rarely incorrect. When you see someone steeple high, accept the fact that this person has a high self image. For nearly forty years, I have seen few exceptions to this interpretation. The only ones I can remember were exceptions because of an injury or disability. But never forget, to see a signal which 'may' mean something gives you power of communication. It gives you power of listening, forgiveness and tolerance. All of these truths are the purposes of this book.

MISTER J.W.: *A STEEPLER WE DECIDED TO SKIP*

J.W. was the name he preferred to be called. My associate and I had an appointment at J. W.'s office to offer our services for an industrial stage show (a Broadway type musical stage show). This company's large sales team would all congregate at some Hawaiian hotel and learn about the next year's products and services (common marketing services in the 60's and 70's).

We met at a luxurious office building in the Washington D.C. area. The office was near the top of the building. We were told to arrive at 9:30AM. At 10:15 we were ushered into the office and the executive apologized. One of our best competitors in this Industrial Show business had already presented their offer. We pretty well knew this company was going to select us or the competing one just interviewed. We had sent in a preliminary proposal and we collectively went over it. In a few minutes this executive began using steepling gestures.

This means he placed his fingers together in a steeple signal and this nonverbal signal was low or in front of his waist. As he spoke, this steepling gesture began to rise upwards until it nearly covered his face. Women rarely do steepling. As a man's steepling rises so does the message of egotism and arrogance. In front of the face it can be the worse type of steepling. When seen it portends to be a major problem for the viewer. It ALWAYS tells the viewer, they have a major ego to deal with.

I tried to ignore this gesture, but it was very difficult. My associate proceeded with most of the presentation as he could see I was not too impressed with the corporate executive. I remained silent and let my associate do most of the talking.

The meeting ended in about a half hour. For me, I wanted nothing to do with this because I thought this executive would be a problem. My colleague had opposite feelings. It was a six figure contract for this industrial stage show. This show would be performed every night for one week with different products highlighted each night. In a word, it was a major event and required a great deal of cooperation and support.

On the plane home my colleague asked what was bothering me. I said I did not want to work with this man as it could be a daily nightmare. I was reminded that it was our best opportunity in six years.

Since I was president of our company, Comco Creative Industries, I decided to pass on this opportunity. This decision soon was known to our competitor who got the bid and show. Their president called me and asked why I had backed out. I did not tell him about the steepling gestures as that wouldn't mean much to him. I did say that the executive probably would be their biggest problem.

The show was produced and our competitor lost over $20,000 on the changes their client made, even up to the last moment. The "steepler" even came to rehearsals daily and made changes. Not all "steeplers" are that difficult to work with, but it is a major nonverbal signal which, for this writer, has never been wrong. If you see steepling just be warned. You have an ego which may be difficult to deal with.

15 THE CHIN UP AS THEY TALK

Have you ever seen someone who talks with their chin up? There could be three reasons for the chin up person. First, they had a neck or back injury which makes it difficult to hold their head level.

Secondly, they unconsciously are mirroring someone in their family. This would now be a habit and NOT a negative signal.

Thirdly, they may have a very high and irresistible belief that they are superior to everyone else. In the movie Gone With The Wind, Scarlet is scolded by her father "Don't stick your chin up at me Scarlet O'Hara." This is a well written line for the signal of pride, selfishness and rudeness.

Chin up people can be a pain in your neck because they want no counsel or advise. With few exceptions, when I see the chin up I know that their ego is up also.

16 EYE STUTTER WITH THE HEAD UP

Eye Stutter is what a person does when they tilt their head way back and blink their eyes very rapidly as they talk. I can only explain this signal since it is difficult to reproduce through an illustration.

I have seen the eye stutter only three times in my life, but in each case the person doing it was lying. So I cautiously offer, the person who you see do this is probably lying. They will tilt their head to avoid eye contact. Their eyes flutter quickly because besides knowing they are lying, they are often looking away while they think of something to say. This internal agitation is mainly manifested in their eyes and nervous hand movements.

Some lesser skilled liars will seem very nervous. This nervousness causes the eyes to stutter. Liars often stutter in speech also. President Richard Nixon did this shortly before he was threatened with impeachment and resigned. He was also lying.

CAUTION: The skilled liar can be as calm as anyone that you've ever seen, and will appear to be very sure of themselves. They almost never tilt their head back and there is almost never any eye stutter.

I once saw a clergyman do it when talking about his own marriage. My reaction at that time was, "He can't be lying, he's a wonderful preacher." Three years later his wife divorced him and the preacher's marital affair of seven years was made public.

17 CROSSED ARMS OVER CHEST WITH HEAD DOWN AND NO EYE CONTACT

I am asked many questions about the meaning of one nonverbal signal or another. I can't count the times I have been asked about crossed arms over the chest. It is true that sometimes it means the person is closed off to you. They have stopped listening and are waiting for the correct moment to leave. YES!

But when their arms are crossed, their head is down, no eye contact, and they look bored, they may be in a comfort zone.

18 HOW SOMEONE SITS IN A CHAIR MAY OFFER IMPORTANT INFORMATION

Where a person sits in a particular chair has a message. In sales training I tell salespeople NEVER try to close a sale – (it's okay to talk to them) but don't make your closing pitch while the prospect is swallowed by their chair. WAIT until they have moved away from the back of the chair.

When someone is swallowed by a chair, meaning they are sitting way back in the chair…NOT on the edge, their nonverbal message is probably one of comfort and not too meaningful. However, they are so comfortable they might not be good listeners at that moment. If you were speaking about something very important, this signal would give you a potential red flag that they are not listening too closely.

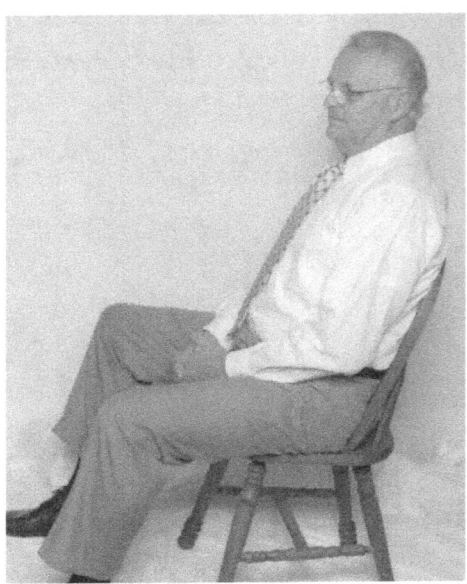

If you were in a sales situation, neither you nor the prospect should look as comfortable as this photo shows.

In selling situations where the prospect sits can be extremely important. Many sales are lost when the salesperson doesn't' notice that the prospect is swallowed by the chair. If and when the prospect moves to the edge ask for the order. He likely wants it. I have so many examples of this counsel I will refrain from adding another anecdote.

If the same person moves to the edge of the chair, this (most often) is an important nonverbal message...even a significant nonverbal message. This move may mean they have connected to what you are saying. They are more interested, even that they are willing to accept some point of view, even to purchase a product you are pitching. This move to the edge of the chair is one way of getting closer and being joined in some agreement with the other person...almost to say everything's fine or I will take it. It works.

Some people often sit at an angle, clearly turning away a from the person they are talking to. Most do it unconsciously, but some do it deliberately. Barbara Walters often does it when she is in disagreement or simply doesn't like the person she is interviewing. I believe if she were told not to turn at an angle she would probably not do it, but the message to many people is one which says, "I don't like you or don't want to be too close to you." Angles create arrogant feelings.

CHAPTER 22

POLITICS AND THE MAJOR
WIN/LOSE SIGNALS

Since the Harry S. Truman/Thomas Dewey 1948 TV debates for the presidency were held in Philadelphia for the first time, television has played a major role in determining who wins the election. The Truman/Dewey debates had little effect nation-wide because at that time only the northeastern section of the country had television sets. However, by 1960 everyone was watching their own television at home. When little known John F. Kennedy ran against the very well known Richard Nixon, it was their television debate which settled the contest. Nixon was far more experienced in politics and, to some, the likely winner.

Excepting local politics where issues seem more important, winners in US Senatorial and especially presidential elections can almost be predicted by nonverbalists after 15 minutes of watching their nonverbal signals AND measuring their facial countenance and ability to speak well on television. Good to excellent countenance and the gift to communicate for political candidates is the best ingredient for winning. Charisma is another word for this good built-in television presence. As Bill O'Reilly of Fox News says, "Charisma is what you're born with. You can't get in college or taking seminars." I agree! With all things being relatively equal, those who have it win! Those who don't, don't. Presidential candidate John McCain did not have it. He even lacked energy and appeared to be a few blinks away from asleep. It was an over whelming win for Obama.

If you are thinking about running for a major office such as a State Representative or US Congress, make sure your countenance on TV is better than your opponents. Those with great countenances win.

John F. Kennedy, the democratic nominee for the presidency had a great countenance and was far less experienced in politics than his opponent, Richard Nixon. Kennedy won the election because of the TV debates. Kennedy looked cool, calm, handsome and articulate; Nixon had bad luck. He had a knee injury and many times he was holding his knee when the camera was supposed to be on Kennedy. Nixon wore a light colored suit while Kennedy looked more presidential in his dark blue suit. Kennedy had taken a few days off to prepare fore the debate. Nixon had campaigned all the day before. He was tired and had lost weight which showed. Nixon's shirt collar was too loose. Even his suit looked loose on him. Nixon had used an after shave powder stick and because the klieg lights were so hot, his sweat washed most of it off making it looked like he hadn't shaved. The powder even streaked in places. It made Nixon look like he was wearing makeup. Kennedy was wearing makeup, but no one could see it. When Nixon spoke, Kennedy wrote notes. When Kennedy spoke, Nixon gripped the rostrum because of his painful knee. Nixon looked sweaty, nervous, tenuous and calculating. For this writer, watching the debates, it was clear Kennedy had beaten Nixon in the debates on television.

Political pundits on the radio thought Nixon had won by an over whelming margin.[1]

Years later in Los Angeles, a number of nonverbalists were gathered for a private seminar. On the hotel television was the first debate between eleven men who were seeking the Democratic Presidential nomination. Our nonverbal seminar leader turned the sound off and asked all of us to watch these debates for a few minutes and pick the strongest candidate based upon their nonverbal signals. Remember, the sound was *off*.

About 40 minutes later our leader asked for our choices. Every one in this seminar wrote down, "the man on the left…the one from Georgia…the guy who is governor in the south. NOBODY knew his name; WE HAD ALL WRITTEN SOMETHING WHICH MEANT JIMMY CARTER at lease 15 months before the election. I add that Carter was way down in the polls at that particular moment; so far down that most people at the seminar were positive he had a major battle and nobody thought he could win, in spite of his superior TV presence. Carter had the best TV countenance and won the nomination.

---

1   *Making of the President*, Theodore, White, Barnes and Noble 2004, p. 340-354

THANKS PRESIDENT CLINTON

I like President Clinton and am extremely grateful for all his wonderful nonverbal signals, even a small dictionary of nonverbal signals… of which some contradicted his verbal messages.

There are plenty of us who don't want to be *talked to* by some people and it is very common to give the signal of angle to that speaker. President Bill Clinton does it frequently when he is confronted with an adept news reporter and doesn't want to answer the question. To hide himself, President Clinton often appears to be hugging himself in an unconscious way of avoiding tough questions. In one interview Clinton did NOT want to be in a room where a newspaper reporter was asking tough questions. He was extremely uncomfortable. His nonverbal signals are shown in next photo.

President Bill Clinton is rarely trapped by an interviewer; he controls almost every interview. When someone tightly squeezes their chest together, pulls their shoulders tightly inward, stands at the angle…and lowers their head, they are trying to hide themselves to be less vulnerable. When he was in obvious control of a public situation he would stand face-front, arms outstretched, palms open as if to say, I'm in control…nothing can hurt me…bring it on. He was making his belly and frontal position open and vulnerable…respectfully adding, just like dogs who turn their belly up to their master.

No politician since Clinton has given such reassuring and powerful messages in his nonverbal cluster signals. When he was obviously in the limelight, but second banana to his wife when she was running for president, he would open his mouth wide and then turned slightly away from his wife as if he was listening.

One nonverbal friend of this writer, says he shows contempt to his wife when he is required to play a secondary role in a joint public meeting. President Clinton had all the nonverbal clusters to agree with this comment, but I am not as certain he was doing it consciously. His mouth would remain open for several minutes as he tried to look relaxed and unaffected by the attention given to someone else. Thank you President Clinton. You were and are a great laboratory of signals – most conflicting with your words.

Another nonverbal Clintonism was when he was facing the world to either 'own up' or 'lie' about his well known affair. The President used the angle position; the head lowered and the pointing finger as a parent would do to admonish a child. He did this nonverbal cluster while his verbal message was "I did not have sexual relations with that woman." Sorry Mr. President, your nonverbal message was louder than you verbal one. It didn't take long for the truth to confirm his nonverbal message…a cluster of dishonesty. He also pointed at the TV listeners to give 'power' to his lie. He may have fooled some, but only those who refused to believe the accusers.

To give a balanced nonverbal picture of President Clinton, he ranks among the best communicators in our century! Only Presidents Reagan, President Kennedy and President Obama equal his great communication ability. In the campaign to win the nomination, Clinton's nonverbal non-endorsement of Obama was a classic nonverbal denial of his expressed support. I wonder how many saw this.

POLITICIANS AND NONVERBAL SIGNALS

Politicians are notorious for lying or giving 'almost truths' to win votes and stay out of trouble on sensitive issues. Nonverbalists have become extremely important consultants in the world of politics. They coach candidates on how to avoid the negative nonverbal messages and more importantly, how to produce positive nonverbal messages. Presidents Clinton, Reagan and Kennedy did not need any manipulation experts. President Obama is an excellent speaker and knows how to play an audience, but his nonverbal persona seems contrived; slightly show business-like. He is more focused on "how he looks."

When Gore ran against Bush in 2004, I was giving a nonverbal seminar in Louisville, Kentucky. It was 11 months before the national election in November. I was asked who would win based upon my nonverbal experience. Incidentally, Bush was NOT very well liked, had extremely poor communication skills and he had a childish laugh he couldn't control, but he was also the incumbent. His TV presence was bad. Gore was winning most polls and was untainted, without baggage and (for his reasons) kept the popular, charming and very strong communicator Bill Clinton out of his campaign.

So what was my answer? I said, "Neither are very good communicators, but Bush is slightly better on TV. Bush should win, but it will be a squeaker." Little did I know.

If you are ever counseling people to run for political office, find out how they look on TV, or get a consultant in nonverbal communication. Those who have a good or better TV countenance usually win.

CHAPTER 23

REMEMBERING NAMES AT A PARTY

How to remember everyone's name at a cocktail party is everybody's problem. The biggest reason why we don't remember a name two seconds after we have been introduced to a stranger is the powerful eye contact we have just received. It is so powerful it turns off our listening. When we meet someone new we almost always look at them in their eyes (where we should look), but this usually interferes with our hearing and we didn't get their name too well.

MEMORY TRICK TO HELP REMEMBER NAMES

The following memory 'trick' has worked for me in magic routines and at parties many times. In fact I was challenged before a party once to see if I could remember approximately 60 new names I would meet at a reception given me after one of my nonverbal seminars. I named 49 people and didn't have to go further, it works.

Here's how it works:

At the precise moment you are given their name for the first time DO NOT look at their eyes. Quickly move your eyes to their shoulders, earlobe, tie or anything except their eyes. Remember eye contact shuts OFF hearing…at least the first time. Immediately repeat their name in your head as you look very closely at them trying to find some odd, different or outlandish item. Pick out something you can characterize with your own silly or distinguishing **head picture**. For an example. I am introduced to a redhead who has many freckles on her face. Her name is June.

I then make up something nonsensical, odd, or a wild exaggeration such as: *June's freckles are falling off* = the **head picture** to remember.

Or *She has freckles only in the month of June.* I repeat my exaggeration several times looking closely at June as I say her name out loud at least two times before I move away. My head picture of June almost always sticks in my head. And believe it or not, your head picture will stay in your head several days or weeks.

When you see the same redhead with freckles again, you probably will think, "she gets these freckles in June, so her name is June." You're safe to say, "It was nice to meet you June." June will say thank you and think, "He remembered my name...wow...what's his name?" It works. Make sure your head picture is reasonable. Don't do what I did once, "It was nice to meet you Miss Freckles."

CHAPTER 24

TWO NONVERBAL SYMBOLS FOR YOUR SUCCESS

What has a tree in a parking lot got to do with you and your success? If we were like this tree we would rarely fail at our tasks, assignments, hopes and desires for advancement and success. This single tree alone in an abandoned shopping mall parking lot produces a very strong without-the-body nonverbal message. I hope it does for you.

In order for this little tree to prosper and grow up through an asphalt pavement, it had to struggle. It had to stay focused and never give up seeking water. Be that tenacious and your life will prosper.

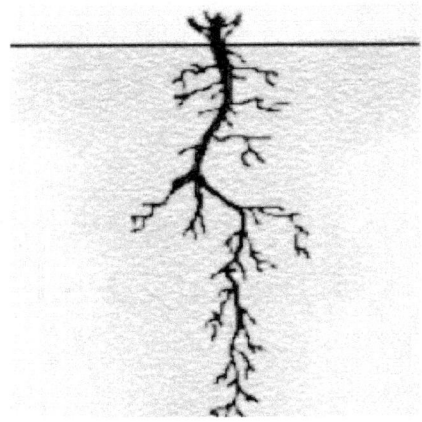

Most plants have tap roots which seek water below…sometimes deep below. Until this tap root finds water the plant could not grow or blossom. I CALL THIS A METAPHOR FOR SUCCESS. Keep focused on your dream, and your hope. Find the tenacity to keep focused on the things you need to achieve success. Symbolically, find the ingredients or skills to move up a little every day toward your life's ambition. Stay focused. Don't give up. Use your figurative 'tap root' and stay focused until you find success.

What has the Space Shuttle have to do with your life's success? It's a nonverbal symbol for this author. Our country figured out how to build a rocket, place a man in it fly it to the moon, land on the moon, walk on the moon AND return safely. A million or more tasks were successfully accomplished one at a time and in a pre-planned sequence for this mission to have succeeded. The number of tasks successfully completed by men probably was in the thousands. Landing on the moon was a major accomplishment, one which required enormous technology. But, the most important reason may have been a simple procedure of operation.

DEBRIEFING EVERY TASK IS THE SOLE REASON FOR SUCCESS

After every single task or group assignment, every astronaut involved would gather together and go over every task from simple to complex and ask what was done, what could have made the tasks better or more successful. How could it have been more or less dangerous? Could they have done it less expensively? What needs to be redesigned and why? If the assignment took only two minutes, each member of the team joined together to 'debrief' every detail of each assignment.

The Space Shuttle success represents my nonverbal symbolism called 'debriefing' and that all seems verbal. It isn't. Talking to a former mission employee, he said many of the 'post mission' examinations were verbal as well as nonverbal. He said, "The astronauts, engineers, technicians, communication specialists, right down to the janitors who had been educated and trained, reviewed, analyzed, studied, and debriefed on every action, step and plan to determine where they could be better.

Think of your own life. By debriefing your daily tasks, you should always see a better way, a safer way, a more compassionate way, a friendlier way, a smarter way, a more productive way for better results. The people I know who do or did this are and were extremely successful and better team players PERIOD! In Kemmons Wilson's book, which exemplifies this 'space shuttle' approach, Mr. Wilson also used a garden metaphor or a nonverbal approach to success, which he followed all his 82 years. I quote from his book, "For best results, your garden should be planted everyday...rows of 'p'eas': Preparedness, Perseverance, Politeness and Prayer...rows of squash: Squash Gossip, Squash Criticism, Squash Indifference...rows of lettuce: let us Love one another, let us be Loyal, let us be Unselfish, let us be Truthful...rows of turnips: turn up for Church, turn up with New Ideas, turn up with the determination to Do a Better Job Tomorrow than you did today." For this writer, this is a nonverbal approach to better living and a better life.[1]

---

1   *Half Luck and Half Brains*, Kemmons Wilson, Hambleton Hill Publishers, 1996

CHAPTER 25

CAN WE SEE A NONVERBAL LIE?

Lying is full of nonverbal signals! Probably the most interesting study about people lying came from Robert Feldman at the University of Massachusetts in Amherst. He studied 121 couples as they had a conversation with a third person. Overall, Feldman found that 90 percent of his participants told an average of two to three lies every ten minutes.[1] James Patterson, author of "The Day America Told the Truth", interviewed over two thousand Americans and found that 91 percent lied regularly at home and at work.[2] As stated in Chapter 10 some of us can get a message that the other person is lying by the person's countenance.

People who only occasionally lie usually use a cluster of nonverbal signals when lying. They include backing the body away slightly, looking

1   The Definitive Book of Body Language, Allan Pease, Bantam Dell, Div. of Random House, Inc. NY, NY, p. 150
2   Ibid p. 149

everywhere except at the person their talking to, lowering the voice or increasing the volume of the voice to make their point stronger. These are common signals of nonverbal question marks connected to their verbal messages.

Pathological or chronic liars RARELY give off a cluster of nonverbal signals. These professional liars are experts in facial manipulation. They can control their signals extremely well and look a person right in the eye with supporting facial nonverbal signals as they are lying. These supporting nonverbal signals usually are nodding of their head, widening their eyes and rocking the shoulders all to confirm their lying. Nonverbal researchers agree that it is extremely difficult even for these experts to know if they are lying. People who claim to be able to identify liars with high accuracy are most likely misinformed.[3] Highly skilled liars usually do not feel guilty about the lie and have convinced themselves that they are not lying or are confident that the target of their lies will believe them.[4]

Many young people convince themselves so thoroughly about something which is false that is true; they can make a solid convincing nonverbal message to support a total lie. Many older adults can't do this as well.

The answer to the chapter question is yes and no. We can and cannot see a lie nonverbally. With pathological liars, these people may give signals they are lying, but some can outwit the best.

Here are the added expression and signals you should be able to identify. For these pictures I will give you my opinion. Remember, an expression is worth many words and meanings…some true.

---

3   Ibid p. 134
4   Ibid p. 134

"That doesn't make sense!"

"That's really neat."

"Let me think about that."

"Sure I believe that."

"Do you think I believe that?"

"You oughta be ashamed."

"You make me sick!"

"That is really cute."

"What's that smell?"

"The dumbest thing I ever heard."

"What did you say?"

"Give me a break!"

"You better not do that."

"You did what?"

"Change that kid's diaper."

"Ahh shut up!"

"What a lame brain."

"I don't want to hear any more!"

"Let me think about that."

"I can't remember."

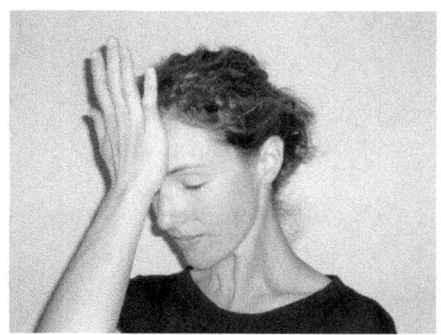

"Why did I say that?"

"The stock market did what?"

CONCLUSION

Begin studying the nonverbal signals you see. There are many more communicated messages you are receiving when you are talking with someone than you can count, figure out or need to worry about. But, each signal you can see and understand WILL give you communication power. If you gain a better power of communication, this book was worth the effort and let it be said, this entire book was written without one word either being spoken or heard. Thanks and keep your eyes open.

INDEX